MW00453309

Experience...
The RADIAC®

PREFACE

Some of this book is a compilation of the Edgar Cayce Readings on a specific subject. The Radio-Active Appliance (now known and available as the RADIAC®) is for individuals seeking to improve their mental, physical and spiritual well being.

Some of the contributions to this book were provided by Joseph Myers. We are very grateful to Joseph for his dedication to this work.

Another section of this book includes articles written by authors who were interested in the RADIAC and the Edgar Cayce Readings.

You will also find some of the many testimonials we receive from those who are amazed, inspired, and changed by their experiences with the RADIAC.

RADIAC is pronounced ray-dee-ack

Please join us at radiac.org for the latest news, research and modern applications for the RADIAC.

BAAR PRODUCTS, INC.
PO Box 60
Downingtown, PA 19335 USA
www.baar.com

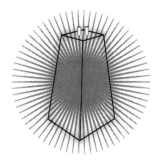

TABLE OF CONTENTS

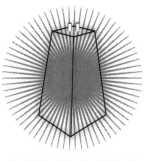

INTRODUCTION

Edgar Cayce died at the age of 67 at Virginia Beach, Virginia, in the year 1945. The records of his Readings are the cornerstone upon which The Association for Research and Enlightenment has been established. These records contain nearly 15,000 pages of single-space typewritten sheets of information recorded by a stenographer in the presence of several witnesses.

The information Cayce covered is said to embrace every subject of common interest to man. Those who came to Cayce sought advice to alleviate illness and pain, overcome confusion in their personal relationships, improve their financial situations, inquire about historical events, and seek guidance regarding future events.

For illnesses, Cayce could diagnose and suggest therapies catered to the health and healing of specific individuals with great detail, regardless of personal familiarity, physical distance, or time; he possessed strikingly remarkable intuition. This capacity to help people popularized Cayce's name far and wide, resulting in countless requests for personal readings. Many of Cayce's Readings on health instructed individuals to utilize specific formulas. Offering an expanding list of those formulas and mixtures, Baar Products, Inc. is the World Wide Official Supplier of Edgar Cayce Health Care. The astonishing accuracy of his diagnoses and the effectiveness of his treatments have been documented at Baar Products, Inc. and this research continues in an endeavor to further understand Cayce's timeless wisdom and practical suggestions.

Cayce's Readings on health include simple suggestions that each of us can follow to stay well. These basic principles included concepts such as a well-balanced diet, regular exercise, the role of attitudes and emotions, the importance of relaxation and recreation, and cleanliness of our physical bodies both on the outside and the inside. The nature of his recommendations indicates that Cayce's understanding of physical care was distinctly ahead of its time. While Cayce's approach to staying well had its roots in health maintenance and preventative medicine, he saw total health as purposeful coordination among the physical, mental, and spiritual components of life.

A complete approach to health must consider an individual's entire being rather than merely the illness itself. Through this perspective, it can be said that the origins of present-day holistic health care are influenced by the Readings of Edgar Cayce.

In over 1,000 Readings pertaining to many different health issues, Cayce gave instructions for the use of an appliance he called the Radio-Active Appliance. Today, that device is called the RADIAC® to ensure its quality and proper manufacture and to eliminate any confusion with the term "radioactive."

At Baar Products, Inc., our objective is to make the information on the RADIAC® available to the public so that individuals may undertake personal research, discover the merits of the device for themselves, and contribute their experiences to the data needed to corroborate the information given in the Cayce Readings. Should Cayce's statements regarding the RADIAC® be accurate, such research may prove itself invaluable to mankind.

Therefore, to continue the research on the RADIAC®, it is extremely important that your personal experiences, no matter how seemingly insignificant, be written down on paper, signed, dated, and sent or emailed to:

Bruce Baar, MS, ND
Radiac Research Project
P.O. Box 60
Downingtown, PA 19335
info@baar.com

Please note, when collecting information or research for the appliance, it is also important to consider the regulations of the Federal Food and Drug Administration. Congress has legislated devices labeled for medical use must provide sufficient data and research to substantiate any claims made for its use. It is for this reason that at this time the information presented within these pages is intended for educational and research uses ONLY. Thank you for your interest, and I look forward to hearing from you.

Bruce Baar, M.S., N.D.

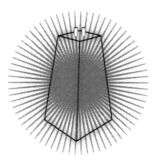

CAYCE QUOTES

ADVICE FOR RADIAC® RESEARCHERS

In general, a Reading was intended for a specific individual. Just how universally applicable Edgar Cayce's remarks may be taken must be decided by each person. A specific application given for one person may be entirely inappropriate for another.

For purposes of clarification, the wording of some selections from the Readings have been paraphrased. Only the selections enclosed in quotation marks are direct quotes from the Readings. The numbers shown are the file reference numbers of the Cayce Readings as found in the library at the Association for Research and Enlightenment at Virginia Beach, Virginia.

HOW THE RADIAC®, RADIO-ACTIVE APPLIANCE OPERATES

Some of the following statements are not direct quotes but have been paraphrased from the Readings as noted. Quotation marks enclose direct quotes.

The RADIAC is not magical, nor does it operate through the imagination, but when properly constructed corresponds to the laws of physics. While they are seemingly of little or no use from outward appearance, their constructive forces are in an orderly manner. This enables quieting from within, and allows constructive forces to predominate and vitalize the system. (957-3)

The RADIAC acts through the relationship between the vibration of certain metals and elements, and the human organism. Metal produces a form of electronic vibration, which becomes a form of motion for the body. Each atom, element and organ of the human body has its own electronic vibration, all of which are necessary for the equilibrium and sustenance of that body. Each bodily unit is a unit of life. It has the capacity for reproducing itself by division. When any organ becomes deficient in its ability to reproduce itself, and maintain the necessary equilibrium for sustaining the physical existence, what it lacks is the necessary electronic energy. These deficiencies may come in many ways: through injury, reaction to internal or external forces, lack of proper elimination, or other lacks. (1800-4)

"... for with any condition that becomes abnormal in the human body, it, the condition, is the lack of an equilibrium produced by the lack of that necessary to produce that vibration in that portion of the organism of the human body that becomes distressed or dis-eased, see?" (1800-10)

The RADIAC is a battery formed of carbon steel which becomes electronized by ice, cold, or water, and then partakes of the same vibrations which form the human body. The connection between man's vibratory forces and the RADIAC produces an equilibrium in the human body, and this in turn enables the body to relieve any tension caused by a deficiency or excess in itself. It would follow that an excess in one part may be forced to assist the part deficient, by a unison of electronic forces, helping the body to increase its production and gain the perfect equilibrium. This action may be compared to sleep, during which the energies of the whole body are enabled to recuperate. The specific conditions for the use of this appliance would be: any catarrh condition in any portion of the system - whether in the head, throat, nasal passages, ears, lungs, stomach, liver, kidneys or urinary organs. And the body is more prone to this catarrh condition than to any other which may exist in the bodily forces. The RADIAC would also be beneficial for any condition bordering on these, in which the eliminative systems produce a symptom. Some of the following are examples: early forms of rheumatism, neuralgia, and headaches. This RADIAC acts as an equalizer yet only to the same degree which normal rest generates recuperative powers in the body. The action, then, is preventative rather than curative except insofar as the body assists through its mental forces, appetite and other rebuilding forces. (1800-4)

"...As given, this, we find, would act as Universal Forces, as would be changed according to the conditions of the system..."(1800-6)

"As we find, all energy is electrical in its activity in a manifested form." (735-1)

"The lowest form of electrical vibration *is* the basis of life." (444-2)

"It has been given again and again; those that are the lowest form of electrical forces that move as energies from the etheronic forces - or of the lowest form of static, or the electrical creative forces. The Radio-Active Appliance, to the extremities." (681-2)

Speaking of high-frequency treatment: "The application of the Radio-Active Appliance is just the opposite end of electrical forces which create that which is the basis of life. For while electrical forces are life in its activity, in man - save where they are to destroy the plasms [sic] that work upon the body itself, they are more helpful in the low form than the high form." (680-1)

"This Appliance is not electrical save by the changing of the vibratory forces from the bodily sources themselves." (1480-1)

"In the Radio-Active Appliance the body builds the charge to be discharged through the instrument into other portions of the body." (1800-28)

"Just as a battery may be charged or discharged, so may the human body be recharged by the production of coordination in a low form of battery reaction, or that as may be given through that of the Radio-Active Appliance..." (5428-1)

"For, as the vibrations are controlled throughout the activity of the Radio-Active Appliance, this takes energies in portions of the body, builds up and discharges body electrical energies that revivify portions of the body where there is a lack of energies stored." (3105-1)

"There is nothing in the Appliance of itself. For, know, as you are told in the Book, in the Law, all that is within heaven and earth, as well as hell, is within the body of the living individual. To cause same to respond to those vibration cells of creative energies, so that each corpuscle of the building of the staying, or of the resisting variety, is aware of its purpose to renew itself, may *best* be attained from its own source of supply, which is within. The activity of the Appliance, then, is to build that low form of energy (which is electrical in itself) as to build up in one extremity and discharge in the other." (3119-1)

"For as the body breaks down the activities by exercises mental or physical, there are used energies - yet not *all* are active; for the muscular forces indicate that unless all coordinate one with another these then produce a fag in some portion of the body - but is the rest of the body worked down. As is indicated by the very principle upon which this acts, then, these produce that in the body itself that will resuscitate and revive same." (1800-28)

"The effect is to keep the circulatory system balanced between the sympathetic and cerebrospinal, stimulating the glands along the whole system where there is the cross activity of the vibrations of the body; creating a more normal balance, giving strength and enabling the body to rest better, thus enabling better mental and physical activities of the body." (478-3)

"...bringing the better metabolism, which is the basic first of all disorders within a living organism, for with a correct metabolism, the body becomes a *normal* outflow, a normal vibratory force, see?" (1800-14)

"These vibrations then add only a better influence in keeping coordination between the superficial circulation and the deeper circulations of the body, and in producing rest and relaxation for the body itself." (1291-1)

"While the Radio-Active Appliance is non-electrical in its reaction, it does produce the proper coordination in the upper and lower portion of the circulation; thus is conductive to rest and ease...not electrical but body balancing!" (515-1)

"Not as a creative, but as a cooperative force." (5425-1)

"How does this act upon the system, by the plain application of a vibratory force to the extremities of the system? In building up any electronic energy (for life is electrical in its activity, materially), and in the forces as are created in that as is applied in same, builds up both from capillary and centrifugal forces as are exercised in the building up of the change in the vibratory ratio of iron and of that builded in carbon and charcoal, and in the electronic influences created in the temperature. In these applications to the body, these take *from* and add *to*, in their respective vibratory forces." (240-1)

"When in accord, that is, all the connections made properly*, or kept so - is the life of use of same; there is no ending. Is there an ending to life, an ending in vibration? It is vibration that is created." (5510-2)

Today, the RADIAC® Radio-Active Appliance is designed to last a life-time. Single Seal Technology™ eliminated leaking found in the older units. See chapter on **Old Radial Appliances: Design Flaws** *(page 47).*

"There will not be felt any vibration from the Appliance you see; but it builds and discharges as would an electronic energy builder for the system to equalize it through the extremities of the body." (1997-1)

"While there will be little or no effect felt, there will gradually - from such applications - come a change in the activities of the system." (1104-1)

"There will possibly occur no feeling from the use of the Appliance except the feeling of being sleepy. Do go to sleep when this occurs. When the Appliance is used, let this period be devoted to prayer and meditation - not as a period for planning the day's work or other activities, but as a period of resting." (4023-1)

"There will not be experienced any vibration or any reaction from the use of the Appliance until the latter portion of the treatment, for it will gradually change the vibrations of the body." (4031-1)

BENEFITS OF REGULAR USE OF THE RADIAC®

"In the simple form, the vibrations from same are well for every human individual." (1800-15)
"Radio-Active plain is very good; good for everybody!" (631-2)

"The Radio-Active Appliance is good for anyone, and especially for those that tire or need an equalizing of the circulation; which is necessary for anyone that uses the brain a great deal - or that is inactive on the feet as much as is sufficient to keep the proper circulation. Best to use same occasionally." (862-3)

"The use of this consistently will be beneficial to the whole of the system." (1151-5)

"Would be beneficial to all human force of life, under present conditions." (1800-6)

"It will be found to aid the body in every direction." (1765-1)

"With the use of Gold Chloride with the Appliance, the whole body will be improved." (701-1)

"The body will be physically more fit for material activities." (1231-1)

"And if the body were to use for its own physical body the Radio-Active Appliance ...it may keep its body in almost perfect accord for many many many days!" (823-1)

"Revivify the elemental forces that create for energies in the body itself." (720-1)

"The vibration as was given for the body should be given, for these [applications] will produce the equilibrium necessary to bring rest and easiness, and sleep, for the body. These do not produce any improper vibration or over-activity to any portion of the system." (325-11)
"As given respecting the use of the Radio-Active Appliance, the vibrations

created by same are not curatives - these are equalizers, if the body is tired, if the body grows weary, mentally or physically, this will be found to be most beneficial - it is for any body, and it would be extremely well for this body. If there are periods when there is weariness, if there is the tendency for an over nervousness, use same. This only stimulates the activity of the nerve or vibratory forces of the low electrical energies in the system to unify their purposes. Hence we find these are helpful and beneficial ever." (1158-11)

The RADIAC vibrations... "will accord the nerve systems... with the purification of the blood stream itself." (5522-1)

"When the body is tired, depleted, or when there are disturbances in any portion of the system, this should be used again to bring the desired effects in allowing the body to rest, in bringing about the better digestive forces, better circulatory forces and - most of all - a better coordination in the cerebro-spinal and sympathetic system." (593-1)

"The vibrations from the Radio-Active Appliance, properly given, will make for rest that is both helpful and body, blood and nerve building." (1278-7)

"This we find, will throw off that of the heaviness, giving the better coordination between the systems and reducing the pressure as is apparent in the blood supply, easing the heart's action, removing strain and pressure from the base of the brain, preventing the flooding of the system with the blood supply that becomes slowed down in extremities." (327-1)

Cayce suggests that the RADIAC is of great value in normalizing weight. This Reading indicates that this would be true for almost everyone: "The use of the Radio-Active Appliance keeps nearer the normalcy as to weight, if any pressures are removed along the cerebrospinal system. This would be true for most anybody." (877-18)

"This will relieve that tendency of cold feet, that tendency of poor circulation in the extremities." (326-1)

"We find this, as has been given, would prove very beneficial in any condition relating to the vibrationary forces in physical bodies, especially that of first stages of rheumatism, catarrh, or any condition that affects the system regarding the elimination for the body. This we find would be well that everyone use such an appliance, for the system would be improved in every condition that related to the body being kept in attunement." (1800-5)

"And this will be... a type of appliance for bringing rest to the weary, rest to those who have been inclined to depend upon sedatives and narcotics for rest; to those who have been under great periods of stress and strain; to those who seek to find an equalizing influence that will assist them in producing a coordination in their physical and mental beings with the spiritual affluence and effect of its activity of spirituality upon the body physical." (1800-28)

"...will put the body to sleep-and not an active force in the nature of a sedative but equalizing the vibratory forces of the system." (1845-1)

"...tend to make the body able to rest without sediments or sedatives of any kind." (414-2)

"Restlessness, insomnia and irritation will disappear." (1472-2)

"By the third or fourth week there should be a decided change; even from the second day there may be a decided change - in that the body may rest much better when it sleeps." (434-1)

"The Appliance will aid in relieving nervousness." (1110-4)

"These forces will...make for the abilities for the body to quiet self throughout." (1192-6)

"To create a balance in the circulation, both for the nerve and blood supply, we would...use the Radio-Active Appliance." (369-10)

RADIAC makes for "more uniform heating forces - as it were - in the system." (5557-1)

Creates "a better metabolism and catabolism in the system." (688-1)

The RADIAC was suggested in a case of tuberculosis for "better coagulation and more resistance in the blood supply." (5441-1)

"This will give stability and the strength to the system, to bring proper co-ordination and proper resuscitation, for even those of the sensory system, in eyes, keenness of taste, keenness of hearing, will respond to these." (378-1)

"Q. What can I do to improve my hearing?"
"A. ...and especially the vibrations from the Radio-Active Appliance." (326-9)

"There would be a great improvement for the eyes, for the hearing, for the throat condition - that appears at times through cold and congestion, by the use of the Radio-Active Appliance, provided this is used consistently... while this will not make for any external feeling the body will find that the responses to the sensory forces will be materially improved." (416-7)

"We will find that impulse, whether as to that of senility when produced from old age alone or senility as produced by conditions produced in the brain itself; for with the proper manipulations to produce coordination with drainage in the system, as may be given through manipulation os-teopathically, or neuropathically given to the system under various stages, may create for a body almost a new brain, will the patience, the sugges-tion, the activities in the system be carried out..." (1800-16)

TIME AND DURATION OF RADIAC® USE

The following Readings were given by Edgar Cayce when asked about the number of times that the RADIAC should be connected to the body. The amount of time it is to be used depends upon the <u>individual</u>. Some people reported they needed to start out using the RADIAC for 30 minutes or less, then work up to longer times.

"Battery is good whenever used, and it may be used every day or it may be used once or three times each week." (337-19)

"This used whenever the body feels tired, whether it's once a day or twice a day, once a week or once a month." (1291-1)

"Do this if not every day at least three to four times a week for an hour, at the period or about the time the body is ready for retirement." (1196-9)

"This should be applied each evening just before retiring, preferably as the body rests lying prone." (1016-1)

"Use the Radio-Active Appliance as she rests; not as she is trying to sleep, but as she rests before retiring." (325-52)

Apply "as the body rests; not at night, but rests during the day." (5490-1)

The following selections illustrate how Edgar Cayce recommended differ-ent time periods for different individuals. On this matter, a person must use his or her own judgment. A general principle, however, is that if the period of application seems too long, to shorten it and gradually lengthen it to between 30 minutes and one hour.

"Q. How long should it be used?"
"A. For 30 minutes to an hour, dependent upon the feelings or reactions of the body to same." (1469-2)

"Q. How long should the Appliance be used?"
"A. Oh, from 30 minutes to all evening! This doesn't matter so much - the time...; but this would be good for anyone, see? Especially to rest tired businessmen, overtaxed ladies - there are a few." (1800-16)

In one case an individual was told to use the RADIAC no more than ten minutes a day and increase the time periods; another was told to start with twenty minutes and increase five minutes a day; another was told to use it for four hours in every twenty-four, and after ten to twelve days, lessening to one to two hours a day. (1103-5) (758-1) (1767-3) (4775-1)

"Don't try to keep self from going to sleep, but do set the period to awak-en." (1852-3)

"If the body falls asleep with the Appliance on, after the treatment time is up arouse him, take it off, and let him sleep!" (856-1)

"Q. How long should the battery be used each day?"
"A. Until you feel like taking it off! Put it on when you go to bed. When you wake up take it off. But if you go to sleep and leave it on all night, so much the better - just so you don't get it tangled up and break it!" (440-2)

"If this is left on overnight, don't worry about it." (3630-1)

"This, to be sure, would be the most effective to the body taken twice each day rather than taken a full period once each day, and each time circulate or make for changes with the plates about the extremities." (1424-1)

"Whenever there are periods of over tiredness, over-anxiety, the desire on the part of the body to make for real rest, use the Appliance." (1022-1)

"When the emergencies arise, or those dizziness or feelings of swimming in the head, we find that the use of the Radio-Active Appliance would be most helpful for keeping a normal equilibrium." (464-17)

"It would not be necessary to use the Appliance each day, but when there is the inclination for pains through the head - or the quickened circulation - make the attachments." (1651-1)

"Q. Should she continue to use the Appliance and how long and how often?"
"A. As we find, whenever there is a period of over-nervousness -prepare this and use it. When there is not the restlessness, do not use it." (1206-6)

"Would be well at times, when the body it tired, either mentally or physically, to use the Radio-Active Appliance. This is not as a -regular- thing; only when tired or weary or when there's been too great an exercise. This will be found to be restful and helpful for the body." (1113-2)

"...to rest or relax during the day, put it on for a few minutes." (2859-1)

"Take the Radio-Active Appliance to rest the body at any time!" (826-7)

"Then it may be left off or used whenever the body is restless, tired, in pain, or distressed." (1443-1)

"Well, if they are taken the rest of his experience it wouldn't be too long; for they are good for that tired feeling which comes at times from worriment. This is as much a preventative as a cure. If these are desired to be left off at any time it may be done; but their helpfulness when once begun will be easily realized by the body." (1151-2)

"In the case of the Appliance, take for a month, leave off for a couple of weeks, and then take again for another month. Thus we find that the body does not become dependent upon other things outside, other than that ye seek in thy meditations." (1183-2)

CREATE AN IDEAL

"Q. Any spiritual advice?"
"A. Keep that purpose in the healing forces. As all healing must come from the divine, then the faith, the hope, the purpose must be in that divine presence that maketh all things possible." (2302-4)

"As to the mental healing, - know first thine own ideal. What is thy ideal? Is the author of thy ideal founded in spirit? Is it the light? Is it the Maker of all that is in the earth, be it perfect or imperfect - according to what man has done with this opportunities? But He in Himself was perfect, an thus becomes the light, the savior, the way, the truth, the life. That is the ideal; not merely in a spiritual sense.
For if that light is that which may control the spirit force in self, and in the choice self may take, does it not also then in the same sense control the results as will be obtained in its materialization in the affairs and the experiences of the individual? That is the ideal, and the source of all healing. For, as has just been indicated, - body, mind, soul or spirit are one, even as Father, Son and Holy Spirit are one. For, they are the materialization of the concept of a three-dimensional individual entity or soul, or consciousness of an entity.
Thus the answer must be in the sources of supply, and in accord with that spirit that maketh a soul, an entity, at-one with the Creative Forces, or the First Cause, or God. That makes one whole." (2528-2)

CONDITIONS FOR USE SUGGESTED BY CAYCE

CONDITIONS FOR USE SUGGESTED BY CAYCE

The Readings for health conditions by Edgar Cayce suggested many possible applications. For many of them, the RADIAC, Radio-Active Appliance was recommended as part of a protocol. The following list of conditions was compiled from the index of the Readings.

(In Alphabetical Order)

Acromegaly
Adhesions
Allergies
Anemia
Anemia Tendencies
Apoplexy
Apoplexy, After Effects
Arteriosclerosis
Arthritis
Arthritis, Suppurative
Arthritis Tendencies
Assimilations
Assimilations/Eliminations
Asthenia
Blepharitis
Blindness
Blindness, Tendencies
Body-Building
Brain, Concussion and
After-Effects
Brain Lesions
Brain, Softening
Catarrh
Catabolism, Metabolism Incoordination
Children, Abnormal
Circulation
Circulation, Impaired
Circulation, In coordination
Circulation, Lymph
Circulation, Poor
Colds, Congestion
Cysts
Debilitation, General
Dementia Praecox
Diabetes
Diabetes Tendencies
Ears, Deafness
Ears, Running
Eliminations, Incoordination
Eliminations, Poor
Epilepsy
Eyes
Glands
Glands, Incoordination
Glands, Thyroid
Glaucoma
Goiter Tendancies
Headache
Heart
Heart, Enlarged

Hemorrhage
Hypertension
Hypertension Tendancies
Hypotension
Injuries
Injuries, Accident & After Effects
Injuries, Birth & After Effects
Injuries, Spine
Injuries, Spine, After Effects
Injuries, Spine, Coccyx
Insanity
Insanity Tendencies
Kidneys
Kidney, Stones
Lesions
Leukemia
Liver, Kidneys, Incoordination
Locomotion, Ataxia
Locomotion, Impaired
Melancholia
Menopause
Menstruation
Metabolism
Mind
Mind, Memory Poor
Mongolism
Multiple Sclerosis
Nausea
Nerves
Nervous System
Nervous, Incoordination
Nervous Tension
Neuralgia
Neurasthenia
Neuritis
Neuritis, Tendencies
Neurosis

Obesity
Obesity, Tendencies
Palsy, Cerebral
Paralysis
Parkinson's Disease
Pelvic Disorders
Pelvic, Amenorrhea
Pleurisy, After Effects
Possession
Pruritis
Psoriasis
Psychosomatics
Psychosomatics, Spleen
Rejuvenation
Relaxation
Rest
Rheumatism
Sciatica
Senility
Sleep
Spine, Subluxations
Sterility
Streptococcus
Surgery, After Effects
Temperature, Fever &
   After Effects
Tic Douloureux
Tic, Facial
Torticollis
Toxemia
Tuberculosis
Tumors, and Tumors, Lymph
Vaginitis
Venereal Disease
Vertigo

GENERAL DESCRIPTION FOR RADIAC® USE

The following quotes from Cayce Readings give general information for use of the RADIAC® and instructions for the method of charging it before application.

"Apply in a normal, nominal, easy manner - where the body may rest, in pleasant surroundings." (5578-1)

"Of course, the body should rest during the period the Appliance is applied, preferably reclining." (2025-2)

"Of course, the Appliance may be taken at home." (1471-1)

"And let the Appliance be in the ice solution for 15 to 20 minutes before applying to body." (550-8)

"Have more ice than water, and never so much that it becomes closer than an inch or inch and a half of the top of the Appliance." (1173-8)

"Keep the ice in same, but not allowing same to come above or to make for short-circuiting." (531-6)

"Q. In cold weather, may the Appliance just be hung outside and then attached to the body?"
"A. *Always* place in cold or icy water, for the action of water on the elements produces the vibration necessary for body." (1800-5)

"Just so [the container, in which the Appliance is placed] is not metal." (448-2)

"Or applied a few minutes two or three times a day as the body rests - not as it attempts to sleep, but taken before retiring or before the periods of the digestive activity will be found to be very beneficial. Hence it would be kept in such a state or order that is charged by the activity of the cold upon the elements within the battery formation itself, in such a way as to become effective as seen as attached to the body... the battery should be kept - as it were - on charge. When not in use disconnect at the container of the battery, you see, but keep with the ice - or the cold about same, so that when attached it is ready for activity." (403-2)

"Q. Must the body rest after using the Radio-Active Appliance and for how long?"
"A. As we find a rest of about 30 minutes is the most effective way. For the activities of the low electrical vibrations created are to equalize the circulation. Then to become active immediately afterward is like violent exercise just after eating a meal when the circulation is centralized in portions of the system for a definite purpose. Then rest a bit and this makes for more effective activity." (1424-2)

CAYCE WARNINGS

At times Edgar Cayce suggested the use of the RADIAC with a warning:

"You can't use the Radio-Active Appliance and be a good 'cusser' or 'swearer,' - neither can you use it and be a good hater. For it will work as a boomerang to the whole of the nervous system if used in conjunction with such an attitude. It is the coordinating effect of the balancing powers in the nervous system, as related to the mental and physical and spiritual bodies, that becomes active with the use of such an Appliance." (1844-2)

"At first this will tend to irritate rather than to quiet." (2587-1)

"Should this produce nausea...these treatments would be reduced in period - but continued in their activity." (4823-1)

"While this will worry for the first evening or two, but we find it will materially aid." (5473-6)

"Some nausea will be produced by the combination of the vibration of these metals in the system, yet this will be necessary to cleanse the system and re-establish it through the forces in the blood that of the proper vibration." (4659-1)

"At times this is found to have a tendency towards aggravating the body. When it does, remove - rather than forcing self to take." (808-5)

The RADIAC was almost always recommended in combination with other therapies. Among these were osteopathic and chiropractic manipulations, massages, oil rubs, herbal remedies, colonics, diet instructions, packs, hydrotherapy, meditation, and exercise. The following are instructions given when the use of the RADIAC was to be combined with other therapies.

"Do NOT combine Appliance treatment with magnetic osteopathic manipulation. ... There may be the massage, or the general massage over the body, and the use of the low electrical vibration in the Radio-Active Appliance or the magnetic; but do not combine these." (5515-1)

"Also the Radio-Active Appliance will aid in equalizing and making for rest to the body while it is going through stress and strain." (635-6)

Use the RADIAC after other treatments to equalize the system.

"*After* the series of treatments are complete - both the osteopathic and the hydrotherapy - we find that the Radio-Active Appliance would be beneficial; for this uses the electricity of the body to equalize the circulation." (2344-2)

"We would not use the Appliance during the strong use of the other influences." (1268-2)

If the person using the RADIAC was using a sedative, Cayce indicated to gradually decrease its quantity, under the supervision of a physician, as the use of the RADIAC begins to produce a different reaction in the body.

"...producing in the body as to cause accumulations of poisons as do sedatives; though it will be necessary to take a sedative when there are the attacks, but take a hypnotic rather than a narcotic - only under the direction, however, of a physician. Gradually decrease the quantity of this sedative as the Appliance, with the series of the colonic irrigations, begins to produce a different reaction in the body." (4023-1)

"We would not discontinue too suddenly the use of the battery when other treatments are discontinued also. Too great a strain on the body with the reactions that must necessarily ensue." (758-29)

CAYCE'S QUOTES FOR DISC #11 AND #112 ATTACHMENTS

The Readings gave many variations for the attachment of the contact plates, but general instructions for their application may be derived from the following excerpts.

"Plates must be in perfect contact with body, not just touching but against the body." (1800-25)

"Keep the anodes or plates very clean. Attach so that they do not cut off the circulation, but so that they are in perfect contact with the body." (1141-1)

"Keeping the attachments firm but not so tight as to make for cutting off the reactions from same." (920-8)

"Be careful that the same plate is always attached first." (3288-2)

"Always attach the same anode first. If you attach it otherwise you will only spoil the Appliance and do yourself more harm than good." (3602-1)

QUOTES ON ATTACHMENT FOR GENERAL USE

"This is over those portions of the bursa on the wrist or just above the wrist bone, on the ankle on the inside - over the bursa area and just above the ankle bone, see, on the inside." (844-1)

Attach plates "Where the pulsations, or the circulation and the nerve impulses are closest to the exterior portion of the body." (2273-1)

"The attachment would be inside the ankle, you see, just above the ankle bone, where the pulse is felt." (2273-1)

QUOTES ON ROTATING ATTACHMENTS

"Do not make the same attachments for two days in succession." (1451-1)

"The Appliance, to be sure, would be attached to the opposite sides of the body. For how was it of old, when one presented self? 'Take hold upon the horns of the altar from the right hand, upon the left foot; from the right foot, the left hand.' Again we see as but a pattern." (1152-2)

"Circulating the attachments about the body...The first attachment becomes the positive, the last the negative." (1504-1)

There were cases which called for the use of the RADIAC several times a day, and the question of rotation is made clear in the following Readings.

"Changing the attachment with each application, even though used two or three times a day." (2025-2)

"Whether the Appliance is used once a day or once in a week, or every other day, or twice a day, for thirty minutes, be sure the change in attachment is made each time correctly." (1498-1)

"Keep the attachments changing, otherwise, the Appliance...would become really irritating. For there is no such thing that if an application can't help, it can't hurt! Because if it is helpful, misapplied it must be harmful - this is natural!" (1179-3)

QUOTES ON HOW TO CARE FOR YOUR RADIAC®

The vibrations which are ascribed to a functioning RADIAC seem to be of a nature that are presently not detectable. Instructions for the care of the device cannot be justified by scientific theories but should be carefully adhered to by those who seek to derive benefits from its application.

"Q. What directions should be given users that they may keep their applicators in good working order?"
"A. When not in use keep them out of water, and dried, see, in sun, and not ever place on metal, there the forces of the magnetic iron may not lose but may gain, see? Keeping all plates polished, never in contact with either, see? Keeping those, when used in solution, in the way of being cleansed before being used, or polished or rubbed, see, that there may be no short-circuiting." (1800-14)

"Keep all portions...apart when not in use." (1268-2)

There were cases where an individual was making progress with the RADIAC and then took a turn for the worse as the RADIAC became ineffective because the contacts were not cleaned with emery paper before use. According to follow-up Readings, when the contact discs were again properly cleaned, the individual began to recover.

"Keep all very clean, by rubbing off with a cloth and polishing the plates or anodes with emery paper each time before applied to the body." (1215-2)

"Keep the attachment plates clean and polished, before and after using." (2109-1)

"Do polish them a bit more, for the vibrations are such that it tends to form a film on same." (1010-20)

"Keep this very clean, for there is the tendency for the wrist and the ankle to throw off - by the effusion or the radiation - those emanations that will

coat the plates very easily." (1005-16)
"The radial activity of the body in its circulation produces a film upon the plates as they are attached to the body." (2772-4)

"Keep the anodes clear and clean, by polishing them each time before they are attached to body...For the vibrations are from the body and there tends to be the inclination for the cuticle of the skin, or epidermis of same to adhere." (1104-2)

QUOTES ON USING THE VIBRADEX® SOLUTION JAR SET

The Edgar Cayce Readings introduce a unique application of medication through the administration of the vibrations of a compound into the system rather than the compound itself. This is done with a solution jar containing the medication. Readings giving the theory and application of this method are paraphrased in part and quoted directly where noted as follows:

For some conditions, the RADIAC therapy lies in the vibration produced by various chemical compounds in the solution jar, applied electronically to the body. The electronic forces themselves are produced by the action of ice on certain grades of steel. As electronic forces pass through the plates a vibration is set up, the electronic vibration partakes of the chemical through which it passes and is distributed to the body through the solar plexus brain, or from those centers about the umbilicus. The action of the loop in the solution, along with the electronic vibration, creates a certain vibration, and this is thrown down in the reaction. If the body needs the qualities of a particular solution, such as a stimulant of any nature, or a drug of a sympathetic nature, when the solution jar is attached to the negative pole it may add to the vibration of the body helpfully. The properties of the solution (or the effects of the vibration) are gradually conveyed to the system. (1800-5)

The vibration given off by the solution creates that same vibration in the body - acting with the elements in the system to produce it. (1800-16)

The following quotation suggests that the vibration from the solution reminds the body what it is in need of and stimulates it to produce it.

"In the nerve system, the brain is the head, and is the active force through which all the conscious sensory consciousness is received. To see someone eating, for instance, produces the vibration in the salivary gland which arouses the gastric juices of the stomach. One becomes hungry, see? In the central part of the brain, the knowledge of subconscious action in the body is located. The blood, for instance, may become deficient or anemic, then the addition of iron, gold or silver, in the various forms or compounds, adds that very same property through this electronic atomic force, and adds it directly to that portion of the system which creates the stimulus in the building or plasm cell - which in turn has been created in the gland, by the action of the nerve system carrying that variation of deficiency, see?" (1800-6)

In response to a request for a general outline concerning the use of solutions, the Readings gave the following information upon the application and theory with regard to treatments given.

"A-3 That first connected with becomes the positive, the last connected negative. The action, then, of properties as may be transmitted by vibration to the body from medicinal forces would act from the negative vibration, for as we find, the body, physical, is of a circuit, in the form of an eight" (1800-6)

"Q-7 What would the spirits of camphor cure?"

"A-7 Nausea and summer complaints. Any intestinal disturbance." (1800-6)

"Q-4 In attaching a container to the negative pole wire, in which is placed tincture of iron, would the application of this cure anemia?"
"A-4 Cure anemia, even in a virulent or exaggerated state. This would be of necessity be rather the preventive than curative forces, though with the application of this we gradually build that condition in the system to overcome, or add iron to the system, see? Then, in adding that property to the system, the application to body would be in this manner: First attach to arm or leg, see? Then attach the negative wire to a connection of silver in the solution, see?" (1800-6)

"Q-5 Would tincture of iodine cure goiter?"
"A-5 Tincture of iodine cures and prevents goiter. This, as we would find would reduce any condition that affects the ductless glands. Would also prove preventive, in cases first beginning, of appendicitis, or of any condition relating to either thyroid or the appendix." (1800-6)

"Q-6 What would spirits of camphor, silver nitrate and gold chloride each cure?"
"A-6 Silver nitrate is a nerve stimulant, see? Any condition pertaining to the nerve system. Chloride of Gold - any condition wherein there is any form of the condition bearing on rheumatics, or of necessity of rejuvenating any organ of the system showing the delinquency in action, see? Nitrate as is added through the silver solution to central portions (which may be alternated gold and silver) for those of a neurotic condition, even unto neuritis, or any form of condition pertaining to enlarged joints, muscles, tissue, any protuberance as comes to portions of the body." (1800-6)

"Q-8 Would the system absorb the tincture of iron, or merely the vibration as given off by the tincture of iron?"
"A-8 The vibration as given off, which creates that same vibration, giving the action with the elements in the system. Same as is acquired from that of the other forms that may be applied through same to system. As given this, we find, would act as a Universal Force, as would be changed according to the conditions of the system. These should be applied through cold, best if the ice is as created with that of manufacture, see? For this carries

more of that vibration to act with the iron. All vibration carrying, then some form of this nature that adds vibration to the organisms in the system, for all are of the units of a vibratory force. These, as given, may be prepared in commercial quantities and applied to everyone, for it would be beneficial to all human force of life, under present conditions. These, as we see, are of the nature that will prove so beneficial to many as suffer from the various ails of the body. Many of the conditions as are existent in alcoholic stimulants, as have been applied to system, that has destroyed the tissue in central portion of the body, destroyed tissue in the recreative forces, in generatory system, destroyed tissue in other portions of the system, even in the brain itself, give these, and gold or silver, or both, would add and rebuild, rejuvenate, as it were, in the system. Give these, for they are good. We are through." (1800-6)

RADIAC® Starter Kit
Without Solution Jar

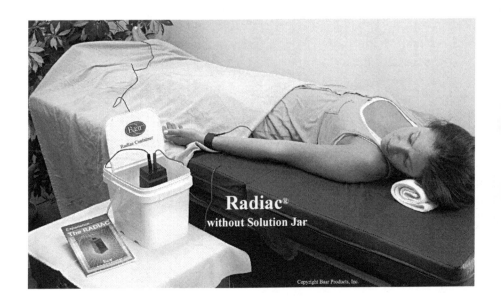

Radiac®
without Solution Jar

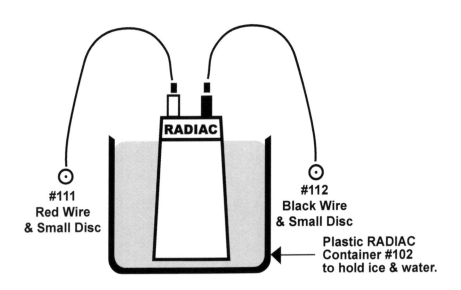

RADIAC

#111
Red Wire
& Small Disc

#112
Black Wire
& Small Disc

Plastic RADIAC
Container #102
to hold ice & water.

RADIAC® Starter Kit
With Vibradex® Solution Jar

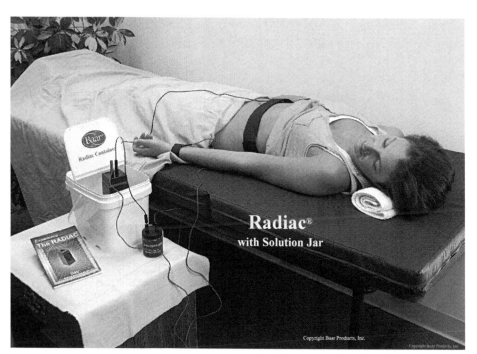

Radiac®
with Solution Jar

Copyright Baar Products, Inc.

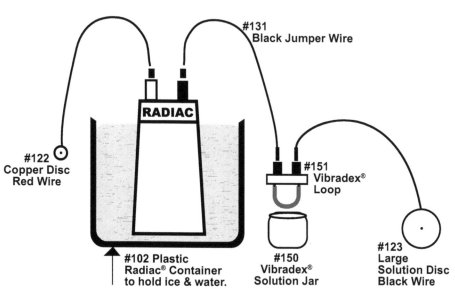

**#131
Black Jumper Wire**

RADIAC

**#122
Copper Disc
Red Wire**

**#151
Vibradex®
Loop**

**#102 Plastic
Radiac® Container
to hold ice & water.**

**#150
Vibradex®
Solution Jar**

**#123
Large
Solution Disc
Black Wire**

QUOTES ON USING THE VIBRADEX® SOLUTIONS

The Readings gave specific instructions for combining application with a solution jar. An overview of some of the Reading excerpts may be found below.

"...and in fevers - always use solution jar arrangement." (1800-16)

When alternating two solutions, do it in such a way that in the course of the cycle both solutions can act from each attachment position on body. (3969-1)

All vibrations enter from the central portions of the body. Best overall attachment is just above and to the left of the umbilicus for the negative plate. (1800-9)

"The first day: Make the first attachment of the small plate to the right wrist, the last attachment - or the larger plate - to the umbilicus and lacteal duct plexus, or three fingers from the navel center toward the right, see?" (1800-11)

"When any condition relating to centralization in body, attach one [negative] to the umbilicus, or just above, or to the right or left, depending on which side of body is needing the condition to be changed." (1800-5)

"When attached for those conditions that use any solution in body, attach the large nickel plate to central portion of body." (1800-9)

"...the larger plate - to the umbilicus and lacteal duct plexus, or three fingers from the navel center toward the right, see?" (1625-1)

"Attach positive plate to other portions of the cerebrospinal system [for certain conditions]." (1800-16)

"As these cause at times apparently over-nerve taxations, by passing directly through the system, we would at this period make the attachment to the extremities of the body." (2155-4)

"Q. Why does the battery have disturbing effect on the stomach?"
"A. This is, then, changed to other centers for its attachments - that will change the vibrations, see? In the attachments of all batteries these should be centralized as those centers from which disturbances radiate, as in those from those pressures to head - may be attached to either in the 1st or 2nd cervical, or just between the eyes, or top of head, and the lower portion of the system. Those from the stomach would come, then, to those of the 4th or 5th dorsal center, and to the extremities." (1000-7)

"Q. When should I begin to use the 10% solution as first directed?"
"A. When sufficient of the poisons have been ridded from the system so as not to cause too quick a reaction in the solution itself upon the metal parts." (1455-2)

"Q. How may we determine when to increase the strength of the solution for this case?"
"A. When there is the lack of the sweat produced by its application." (1800-32)

"In those of conditions as would be found that have to do with any of those conditions as have to do with the typhus, [thymus], or with any of the glands of the throat, and of the glands of the genitive system, or endren [adrenal], or those of any of the head, or those of the throat - these will be found beneficial in these conditions, and will be alterable according to the character of the blood tests, as to whether these change in their formation, see?" (1800-16)

"...let the solution and the anodes be attached for a few minutes before being attached to the body." (1553-22)

"Remove the connection that passes through the solution when it is not in use." (1553-5)

"Only put into the solution when attached to the body, and only attach the anodes to the Appliance when ready for use. Put the Appliance for the temperature change ten to fifteen minutes. When ready to apply to the body, you see, put the carrier into the solution and attach immediately to the body; or attach to the body and then to the solution. Only let the attachments remain 30 minutes. Immediately take same out of the solution, you see, cleanse it; that there may be the perfecting." (1800-32)

"Do not use the same connections for any two solutions. Have separate connections for each solution. These should be taken from the solution when not in use. These should be kept very clean." (3591-1)

"Of course, have separate connections for each Solution. These are not both to be used on the same day, you see, but alternated, one used one day, the other used the next day, and attached in the manner indicated for each." (1769-2)

VIBRADEX® SOLUTIONS RECOMMENDED FOR SPECIFIC AILMENTS

Solutions were occasionally suggested for use with the RADIAC®. Readings identified certain physical and mental difficulties with a deficiency of some element or compound in the body. The following is an overview of the Vibradex® compounds which were recommended for various specific ailments.

Spirits of Camphor:
Nausea, summer complaints, any intestinal disturbance, deafness, nerves (to create strengthening to the muscles and to the muscular tissue in tendon and in muscle - 4501-1), circulation, cerebral palsy, paralysis, assimilations, eliminations.

Spirits of Camphor and Gold Chloride, alternated:
Hypertension, insanity.

Spirits of Camphor and Muriated Iron, alternated:
Incoordination in assimilations and eliminations.

Spirits of Camphor and Silver Nitrate, alternated:
Catarrh.

Gold Chloride:
Rheumatics: "rejuvenating any organ of the system showing delinquency in action." (1800-6), epilepsy, glands, insanity, eliminations, arthritis, melancholia, nervous system, impaired locomotion, torticollis, poliomyelitis, cerebral palsy, possession, lymph circulation, allergies, pelvic disorders.

Gold Chloride and Soda, alternated:
Arthritis.

Gold Chloride and Silver Nitrate, alternated:
Neurotic conditions, senility, neuritis, enlarged joints, muscles, tissue, any protuberance, after effects or birth defects, nerves, "given properly, silver and gold may almost lengthen life to its double." (120-5)

Gold Chloride and Muriated Iron, alternated:
Nerves, insanity.

Tincture of Iodine:
Arthritis, neurasthenia, glands, obesity, toxemia, anemia, for plethora condition in glands, any condition affecting the ductless glands, appendicitis, thyroid, goiter, nervous tension.

Tincture of Iodine and Muriated Iron, alternated:
Nerves.

Tincture of Iodine and Potash, alternated:
Leukemia.

Tincture (or Muriate) of Iron:

Anemia, general debilitation, "Stabilizer for the blood supply" (4440-1), adhesions, lesions, rebuilding nervous system, circulation, toxemia.

Tincture of Iron and Silver Nitrate, alternated:

Neurasthenia.

Silver Nitrate:

Nerve stimulant, nervous system, circulation.

EXAMPLES OF THERAPIES FOR SPECIFIC AILMENTS

The following Readings may suggest directions to take in attempting to research the information contained in the Edgar Cayce files. It is advisable to research the entire Cayce Reading or file which pertains to a particular condition as there may be variations in application.

Alcoholic Stimulants

"Many ills are results of alcoholic stimulants. These have destroyed tissue in the central portions of the body; destroyed tissue in the generative system, in other places and in the brain itself, gold and silver are good for this, they rejuvenate the system." (1800-6)

Alcoholism:

Helps cure body of taste for alcohol. (881-1)

Cerebral Palsy:

Use a solution of Gold Chloride and attach the positive plate to the first or second cervical center and ninth dorsal the next.

Colitis:

Attach to extremities one day, to umbilical center and ninth dorsal the next.

Deafness:

Have the positive as close to the ear as possible, over soft tissue of same, or just back of ear. Keep the positive near the ear, and then alternate the negative between the third dorsal and the ankles. (10-1)

Digestion:

Taken before periods of digestive activity will be found to be very beneficial. (403-2)

Downs Syndrome:

Using the RADIAC with the Gold Chloride solution would materially benefit Downs Syndrome. (1105-1)

Epilepsy:

Use two solutions, one with Silver Nitrate solution and one with Gold Chloride solution. Attach the positive to the first or second cervical.

Impaired Locomotion:

Using a solution of Gold Chloride, attach the POSITIVE to the fourth dorsal plexus and the NEGATIVE (with the solution) to the extremities. (393-1)

For an impaired limb attach the plates only to the injured limb and its opposite, alternating them. (1987-1)

Insomnia:

"Use the Radio-Active Appliance as she rests; not as she is trying to sleep, but as she *rests* before retiring." (325-52)

Leukemia:

Use a solution of Iodine and solution of 40% Potash. Alternate them, with the iodine solution on the negative wire (going to the umbilicus) when the positive is attached to the wrists (going to the umbilicus when the positive is attached to the ankles). (71-3)

Menopause:

Circle the body with the attachments, except a few days before the regular monthly period, when the attachments would be made, first to the last dorsal, the other (the negative) to the pubic center. Continue for a month, or through the full monthly period. Then leave off for a few days and begin again. (1457-1)

Menstrual Cramps:

Positive to fourth lumbar plexus, negative to pubic bone. Start two or three days before and use for duration of the period. (1389-1)

Menstrual Irregularity:

Use normally except a few days before the menstrual flow, attach positive to the twelfth dorsal center, negative to puba bone. (745-1)

Menstruation:

Do not use the RADIAC during the menstrual flow - arrange schedule around menstruation. (3583-1)

Prenatal or Genetive Conditions:

Use a separate RADIAC for Silver Nitrate and Gold. Make one attachment to the extremities and one to area of the first and second cervicals. (1800-16)

Softening of the Brain:

Using a solution of Gold Chloride, attach the positive to the first and second cervicals, the negative to the tenth and eleventh dorsal center. (2104-1)

Subluxation of the Spine:

One day in two or three attach the negative to the third cervical - beside rather than on it. (4767-2)

Torticollis:

Use Gold Chloride and attach the negative to the upper right of the umbilicus, or near the lower left end of the . (5662-1)

Urination:

For frequent and painful urination attach the negative to the lower portion of abdomen and the positive to the ninth dorsal. (601-24)

Vaginitis:

Attach the positive to the fourth lumbar center, the negative to the pubic bone. (538-45)

Use through the body for four days, around the body four days, and rest four days. (538-46)

See page 58 for a list of Vibradex® Solutions.

Single Seal Technology™

SINGLE SEAL TECHNOLOGY™: WHAT IS IT?

Single Seal Technology™ is the process of completely sealing the Radiac® with one material as opposed to using 2 or 3 different materials. It creates the perfect seal and completely protects the Radiac for a lifetime of use. Because of Single Seal Technology, water or moisture is unable to get inside and destroy your Radiac.

Single Seal Technology was developed by Dr. Baar after studying and evaluating years of old, poorly manufactured appliances. Years ago, these old style units (sometimes called Radial Appliances. "Radial" Appliance is a misnomer and today suggests a poorly designed unit) were made without the knowledge of long term consequences, which caused several major problems involving their use and handling.

Numerous incidences were reported of old appliances "whistling," "gurgling/bubbling" and "sucking in air" when in use. These older appliances were created with different materials and welded together to create seams. The normal use of an appliance caused the outside materials to expand then contract at rapid speeds. This resulted when placing it in the sun, which would heat it up, then placing it in a container of ice and water. Here we have 2 different extremes in temperature. The different materi-

---

* The term "Radial Appliance" is a misnomer and quite often used by those unfamiliar with the origin.

als used in the construction combined with the wide differentiation in temperature would cause the outside materials to expand and contract at different rates of speed and separate from each other in the process. This created hairline cracks, sometimes invisible, sometimes quite obvious. The noises and bubbling were a result of air or water being sucked inside of the unit because of the cracks in the seams. Water or moisture would seep into the appliance and ruin it quite easily. These faulty units became defective once these separations occurred. Often times the cracks were so small they were barely visible. See the following images:

These three examples show older units which have separations caused by the use of different materials, which made the appliances ineffective and totally useless.

THE CREATION OF THE SINGLE SEAL TECHNOLOGY

When Dr. Baar began researching this and speaking to individuals whose units were no longer working, he determined that a new process was needed to protect the device and allow it to provide functionality for a lifetime. The development of Single Seal Technology produced the result that would guarantee the Radiac to remain sealed and protected. Because of this, and many other design flaws in the older units, the name Radiac was trademarked to distinguish the attention to detail and design of this technology. It offers customer assurance and protection. This trademark insures that the unit will never break or crack as in the older units and has a Lifetime Guarantee.

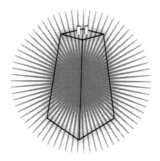

DR. BAAR'S OFFICIAL INSTRUCTIONS FOR USE OF THE RADIAC®

The following is a summary of instructions concerning the general use of the RADIAC®:

1. **DO NOT** ingest alcohol on a day that the RADIAC is used.

2. **DO NOT** place the RADIAC on or near metal or magnets.

3. **ALWAYS** attach #111, Red Wire with Disc, to the body FIRST. When a Solution Jar Set is used with the RADIAC, a different set of wires with discs are used.

4. The RADIAC **CANNOT** be shared among individuals. It must be used by one and the same person only.

5. **NEVER** attempt to repair the wires by soldering.

6. Should the RADIAC break in some way or should someone accidentally use another person's RADIAC then the RADIAC can be sent back to be cleared in certain cases. Contact Baar Products, Inc., at info@baar.com or 610-873-4591 if this occurs.

7. Keep the discs and wires disconnected when not in use, and **DO NOT** let the discs touch each other at <u>any</u> time, whether they are connected to the RADIAC or not.

8. To activate the RADIAC, place it in a plastic or non-metal container, or RADIAC Container #102, filled with ice then add water (using more ice than water). Make sure that the ice and water come up to the red line on the RADIAC which is located just below the top of the RADIAC. The RADIAC should be placed in the ice water for about twenty minutes before making the attachments to the body and continue to remain in the ice water during use. Keep water from entering the insides of the red and black jacks on top of the RADIAC by using the RADIAC Protector Cap #103.

9. Polish (sand) #111 and #112 discs carefully with Emery Paper #153, **before and after** each use. This is crucial to the successful operation of the RADIAC; any film left on the discs will obstruct the circuit of the RADIAC and accomplish nothing.

10. For ordinary use, attach the wires with discs in the following order:

REMEMBER: ALWAYS ATTACH RED WIRE FIRST.

DAY	#111 RED	#112 BLACK
First	Inside Right Wrist	Inside Left Ankle
Second	Inside Left Wrist	Inside Right Ankle
Third	Inside Left Ankle	Inside Right Wrist
Fourth	Inside Right Ankle	Inside Left Wrist

11. Avoid attaching the RADIAC to the same body position twice in succession when circulating around the body. It may be helpful to keep written notes on your last attachment points.

12. Ordinarily, a session can last 30 minutes to one hour, but this should be consistently done - at the same time each day, in pleasant surroundings, remaining quiet, and preferably lying down. It may be helpful to set a

Timer #298, for the allotted time.

13. The RADIAC should be used by following the above four day cycle. One standard suggestion is to use the RADIAC for three cycles of the body (twelve days) then discontinue use for the following four days. Repeat the full sequence.

14. When not in use, keep all parts dry and the RADIAC itself in the sun for an hour or more when practical. Prevent water from entering the jacks by using the RADIAC Protector Cap #103. Do not place the RADIAC near any metal objects.

15. For optimum results, your attitude should be positive, expectant, grateful, reverent and prayerful.

16. It is important to use the device when you <u>feel</u> like it. An urge to use the appliance should be considered as a good indication to do so. Likewise, pay attention to any urge to <u>not</u> use the appliance or to stop using it before the suggested allotted treatment time is up. However, this is not to say that you should use the appliance in a random manner, as the whim suits you, since it is stressed that persistent and consistent treatment times and cycles are best.

USE THE RADIAC® IN THE CORRECT SEQUENCE

1. Place the RADIAC in the RADIAC Container #102. Add ice up to the red line of the RADIAC and then add water up to the same red line. Wait 20 minutes to activate. Be sure that no water splashes inside the red or black jacks by using the Protector Cap #103.

2. Polish #111 and #112 discs with Emery Paper #153 — keeping discs and wires apart at all times. Wipe with a clean cloth.

3. Insert #111, Red Wire with Disc, into the red jack on top of the RADIAC.

4. Now insert #112, Black Wire with Disc, into the black jack on top of the RADIAC.

5. Next, attach the #111, Red Wire Disc, to the proper extremity. Use the Velcro Strap, #142, to secure the disc to the pulse point. (Day One: Attach inside right wrist.) *See page 52.*

6. Now attach #112, Black Disc to the proper extremity. Use #142 Velcro Strap to secure the disc to the pulse point. (Day One: attach inside left ankle.) *See page 52.*

7. Next, lie down and relax in a comfortable, dim, and pleasant room. Keep arms and legs apart. Maintain the proper frame of mind. **REMEMBER: DO NOT ALLOW THE RED AND BLACK WIRES TO TOUCH WHILE USING THE RADIAC.**

8. When the session time of 30 minutes to one hour is complete, remove the <u>Black</u> Wire with Disc from body <u>first</u>, then the <u>Red</u> Wire with Disc. Next, remove the Black Wire from the RADIAC and then the Red Wire from the RADIAC. Finally, remove the RADIAC from the container and towel dry.

TO ATTACH:	TO REMOVE:
1. Red Wire to RADIAC	1. Black Disc from Body
2. Black Wire to RADIAC	2. Red Disc from Body
3. Red Disc to Body	3. Black Wire from RADIAC
4. Black Disc to Body	4. Red Wire from RADIAC
	5. Remove RADIAC from Water and Towel Dry

9. Sit back and rest for another 30 minutes to allow effects to continue. **This is important**.

10. After the **30 minute rest period**, clean the discs with a cloth first and then sand the discs with Emery Paper. Return the wires with discs to separate plastic bags. Store the RADIAC in the sun for at least 1 hour.

RADIAC DISC ROTATION

RADIAC DAY 1

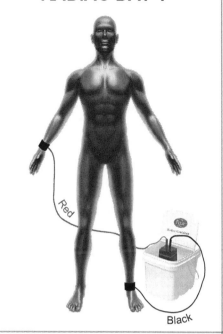

RADIAC DAY 2

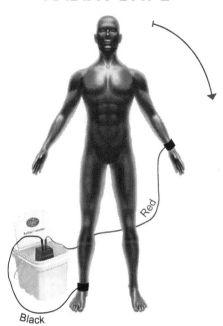

RADIAC DAY 4

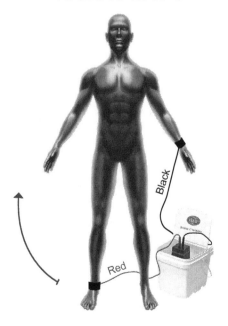

RADIAC DAY 3

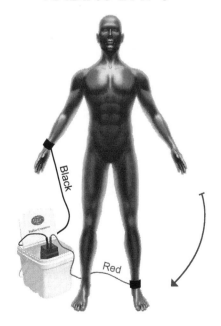

SUMMARY OF RADIAC® USES WITH VIBRADEX® SOLUTIONS

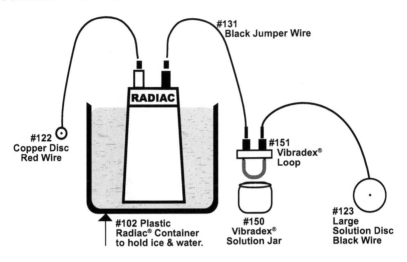

1. **DO NOT** ingest Alcohol on a day that the RADIAC will be used.

2. Make all preparations in the same manner as given in the instructions for general use, except that you use a different set of wires. Product #122, Copper Disc with Red Wire, is used for the first contact and Product #123, Solution Disc Large with Black Wire, is used for the second contact.

3. Place the RADIAC in the RADIAC Container #102. Fill with ice then add water.

4. Remove the Solution Jar Storage Lid and fill the Solution Jar #150 with the selected Vibradex® Solution. Place the Element Wire Assembly, #151 (lid with metal loop attached) in the Solution Jar. **Please Note**: a separate Additional Solution Jar Set, #141, is required for each different type of Vibradex® Solution used. (i.e. one for gold, one for camphor, etc.)

5. Insert #122, Copper Disc with Red Wire, into the red jack on top of the RADIAC.

6. Insert #131, Black Jumper Wire, into the black jack on top of the RADIAC then into one of the black jacks on the Solution Jar Lid.

7. Insert #123, Solution Disc Large with Black Wire, into the open black jack on top of the Solution Jar Lid. Now, wait 5 minutes before attaching the discs to the body.

8. Attach #122, Copper Disc with Red Wire to the body, FIRST. The Copper Disc with Red Wire may be rotated around the extremities - right wrist, left wrist, left ankle, right ankle, with each successive treatment - **Or** - the Red Wire with Copper Disc may be attached to a spinal point. You can use surgical tape to secure the disc to the spinal point.

9. Attach #123, Solution Disc Large with Black Wire, to the navel area. This location point is three fingers to the right of the navel and two fingers up. Use #142 Velcro Strap or surgical tape to secure the Solution Disc Large to the spinal point.

10. Relax and allow the RADIAC to work for 30 minutes to one hour.

11. Remove the wires with discs as noted on page 54. You must rest for 30 minutes after your treatment. Application time should not exceed 60 minutes when using a Solution Jar Set with the RADIAC. Setting a timer is suggested.

12. It is necessary to remove the Element Wire Assembly (loop) in the Solution Jar **immediately** after the session. Place the storage lid on the Solution Jar when not in use.

13. After the 30 minute rest period, rinse the loop carefully under running water. Wear gloves to brush or sand the loop gently while thoroughly removing any residue. Allow it to air dry. **Please note:** The loop should only be immersed in the Vibradex® Solution while an application session is in progress. Some of the solutions used in the Solution Jar will create a residue on the loop after using the RADIAC. There are also colorless solutions (i.e. camphor) that do not form a visible coating on the loop after treatment; nevertheless, the loop must be cleaned.

14. Keep all Vibradex® Solutions in a cool, dark place in order to prevent sunlight from altering the compound.

15. One suggestion for the use of the Solution Jar is to combine its application with the general "no solution" treatment in the following manner:
   (1) A four day cycle with the Solution Jar.
   (2) A four day cycle without the solution.
   (3) A four day rest period.
   (4) Repeat.

VIBRADEX® SOLUTIONS AVAILABLE*

#166 Gold Sodium Solution, 1 grain/oz.
#174 Gold Sodium Solution, 2 grains/oz.
#178 Gold Sodium Solution, 1%, 5 grains/oz.
#154 Gold Chloride Solution, 1 grain/oz.
#181 Gold Chloride Solution, 2 grains/oz.
#155 Gold Chloride Solution, 1%, 5 grains/oz.

#157 Silver Solution, 10%
#158 Silver Solution, 2%
#186 Silver Solution, .66%

#160 Atomic Iodine Solution, 1%
#173 Tincture of Iodine

#156 Camphor Solution (natural)

#159 Tincture of Iron

#185 Baar Lyme Compound Solution

* You may use the same jumper wire for multiple vibradex solutions.
**See baar.com for other solutions.

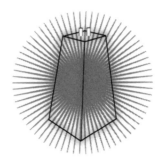

PERSONAL GROWTH USING THE RADIAC®

INDIVIDUAL USE OF THE RADIAC®

There seems to be a strong relationship between the user of the RADIAC and the RADIAC itself. This is not clearly understood today, although there are clear warnings not to use a RADIAC that has been used by someone else. On the basis of the following, our recommendation is that each individual have his personal RADIAC, that has not been, and that never will be used on anyone else.

"Be sure no other body uses the Appliance." (5326-1)

"Do not use an Appliance that has been used by someone else, but have same prepared for this body." (843-10)

"Do not use this Appliance on other than the individual entity to whom it is first applied. For this builds to vibrations." (5158-1)

MENTAL ATTITUDES WHEN USING THE RADIAC®

From a study of the Readings, it appears that the attitude of a user of the RADIAC is all important with regard to the results. Expectancy, reverence, prayer, persistence, gratitude, all seem to be necessary elements which must be contributed by the individual who would benefit from the use of the RADIAC. The following Readings emphasize this and give a warning to those who do not maintain the proper attitude.

"During the whole periods, each evening - as the applications of the Radio-Active Appliance are made...let the parents, in meditation over and with the body, as it begins to slumber, give these: not merely as words, but in their own words, but these as the essence, as the purposes, as the sayings: "The Father of Light and Mercy and Truth, create in this body that as will bring the perfect coordination of the members of the body itself, that the soul may manifest in a perfect body. These we seek through the faith in Thy promises to those who call on Thee, that Thou wilt hear and answer speedily. Thanking Thee for Thy mercy, for Thy care, for Thy love. This we offer in humbleness of Thy name, O God!" These continued daily, these brought to the daily application with others, with thy care, with thy love, will bring help, hope and understanding to all." (1314-2)

The parents were told to give suggestion to their child "together, not separately (for this is your responsibility - you can't shun it - you can't delegate it and get the results yourself)... Then attach the Radio-Active Appliance and as the body goes to sleep, make the suggestions. Then take thy trouble to thy Maker, and in thy suggestions appeal to the Divine within this developing body." (5022-1)

"Make haste, here, slowly. Do not be impatient. Have associations and relationships with others. In doing that, those will aid materially in keeping and in bringing about the healing gained from the Appliance." (758-9)

"Use the Appliance in a sympathetic manner; that is, not as mechanical, but rather as the desire that same create the necessary forces within the... physical forces. These...would bring about a much nearer normalcy for the body." (5640-3)

"Use the Appliance one hour each day, but don't use it one day and then change the hour or use it some other time of day at the next. Be consistent and persistent, and we will bring results." (867-2)

"But if it is done haphazardly it will do no good at all!" (569-3)

"These must never be applied as rote. These must not be used just to get through same, but in each application day by day see and feel constructive reactions taking place. For remember, ever is this a growth in attitude, state of mind..." (867-1)

"In your prayers, not only say that but see it, *know* it is taking place!" (1632-2)

"Be persistent. Be patient. Be *prayerful* as these applications are made." (2169-1)

"Q. Am I using the Appliance properly and is it working all right?"
"A. It has become more mechanical than it is working. It is working in the physical sense, but without expectancy - as in taking anything for the correction of disorders in system, unless the attitudes can be such that these are of an expectancy - little may be accomplished with same...not as rote, but as sincerity of heart, mind and body." (5640-3)

"Q. How often and how much longer should the Radio-Active Appliance be used?"
"A. *If* it is *not* to the advantage of the body that it gives an opportunity for the use of its spiritual balance, leave it off! For it can be made very detrimental! But if it is used at the period for the body to meditate and pray, thus making a better coordination between all of its mental and spiritual and physical forces, the longer it is used the better! Not at one period, of course, but continuously over a long period, for the whole of the mental and spiritual and physical reactions. This is beneficial for *anyone, properly used!* It is harmful, improperly used. You can't use the Radio-Active Appliance and be a good "cusser" or "swearer", - neither can you use it to be a good hater. For it will work as a boomerang to the whole nervous system if used in conjunction with such an attitude." (1844-2)

"For Jesus is the Way and the Light, and in Him is the strength - but not of self-willed nor of an imperfect body [not in attunement]; and not of self-indulgence not of self-glorification not of self-exaltation - but be ye humble even as He. And in doing these, we will find that the better physical and mental attitudes may by thine." (361-8)

USING THE RADIAC® FOR SELF-UNFOLDMENT

The Readings suggest that the use of the RADIAC® may bring a new level of self-realization and unfoldment to those who exercise the will to use it properly. For others, it may enable them to read with new powers of comprehension, and for still others, it may enhance their dream experiences to aid in spiritual awakening.

"Pay attention to the unfoldment of the subconscious self through dreams during the period of the Appliance applications." (911-2)

"If the body goes off to sleep during the period, have someone to remove the plates, but there will be periods of exciting experience in the spiritual and mental self." (5199-1)

Spiritual Readings while using the RADIAC "will not only enable the body to rest, it will enable it mentally to be more active, it will find the general reactions to spiritual influence of quite a different nature." (1245-1)

"Begin to analyze self and the relationship the entity bears with the universe and its Maker. Begin first by reading something from the Book itself. It would be well to read first the first five to six verses of the first chapter of Genesis, and in the third verse understand what it means - that the knowledge is within thine own self, the light necessary for you - to be one of the best men God ever created. For He has promised to be with you, as an individual, if you will be with Him. Then turn to Exodus 19-5 - this is not merely talking to Jews or Hebrews or Israelites - It is talking to (you), then read the 30th chapter of Deuteronomy. Again it is you an individual. Read then the promises in the 14th, 15th, 16th and 17th (chapters) of John. They are not foolishness, my friend! Be a man! Be a man after God's own Heart, not one ashamed but rightly placing the emphasis where it belongs. Study these passages at periods when you have a Radio-Active Appliance tied to you. Read them. Then close thine eyes and visualize it working within thy mind and body. You'll be proud of those about you and yourself." (3432-1)

To a 60 year old woman at the verge of death Edgar Cayce suggested two thirty minute periods of RADIAC treatment each day with someone to read these portions of the Scripture to her: the 23rd, 1st, and 24th Psalms, the 30th of Deuteronomy, the 14th, 15th, 16th and 17th of St. John, the 11th of Hebrews and the 7th of Romans. "Use these periods to begin then meditate, listening for the still small voice within. For it is in thine own temple He has promised to meet thee. These will bring more comfort and more aid than all the medicinal properties." (5311-1)

Use "not while there is the use of the high mental faculties in the study of *problems,* but when there are the relaxing periods. It will relax the body, tone the system." (1481-1)

"However, if through such a period there is required that there be conversation, it is better that the Appliance be used then than not at all." (1040-1)

"But do not attach same and then continue to work the body mentally or to make for conversations that tend to create this flow of the circulation to the mind's activities." (1062-1)

"Know that the help, the aid, must be first mental and within self; and that all healing comes from *constructive*, spiritual forces within self; and that with the changes wrought, these are not to be made for self-aggrandizement, self-indulgences, but that the spirit of truth, of good, of love, of patience, of reproduction, may be fully accomplished; that the body, in mind, in body, in spirit, may fill that for which it came into the material experience in the present." (1389-1)

"As ye apply these suggestions, as ye read, as ye meditate, during the period of the application of the Radio-Active Appliance, do make personal application, practical application of such tenets and truths as ye come out [of meditation] - ye will know that the ability is within self. Do that. Do not trust in forces other than those that are within self. Remember thy body is the temple of the living God. And He promises to meet you. As you attune yourself by the outer circulation the inner circulation [through the use of the vibrations set up in the RADIAC], ye may easily attune the Divine in thee to the Divine that is of the Universal Consciousness. Ye can by the will of self make self in accord. Do it. Live it. Be it." (3384-1)

"The most physician needed is within self. The physician is the Christ-Consciousness." (3384-1)

USING THE RADIAC® WITH MEDITATION

Again and again the Edgar Cayce Readings make it very clear that to use the RADIAC should enable one to experience a closer relationship to his Maker.

"Prayer is supplication to God and meditation is listening to His answer." (2946-6)

"And when the Appliance is attached, use that period for the meditation, or the affirmation as to the body's oneness with the Creative Forces for a purposefulness in manifesting among its associates and fellow men the glory of a *risen* Lord!" (1663-1)

The use of the RADIAC tends "to unify the Coordinating centers from which the physical, the mental, and the spiritual receive their impulse, this becomes a period when the deeper meditation would become more preferable..." (920-12)

"For He knoweth what each hath need of, even before we ask; but by attuning of the vital forces of the body by those energizing experiences of the metals in the Appliance we attune the Infinite within self to the Infinite without." (1211-2)

"This period of its application becomes a season when the attunements can come closer - and closer yet - to that union that creates harmony, peace, hope, energies within the bodily forces themselves." (1390-1)

Use the 24th, the 23rd and the 91st Psalms. "Learn these and use them for the meditations, and we will bring peace and harmony for this body." (3366-1)

"...use that period, when the Appliance is attached, for meditation; when the body would meditate upon its purpose in the earth, its thanks and praise for the living God; its desires to be the channel for a blessing, for a helpful experience, for the knowledge of God in the life and experience of others." (2800-1)

"And make this 30 minute period each day as the period of meditation. Let the meditation be put in the body's own words, but following as this: Great Creative Forces, I am Thy servant, and would give myself in body, in mind, in spirit, to the service of my fellow man that the Creative Forces may be the better understood, and man's relationship to same known in the heart of men. Make Thou, then, my body *whole*, in the ways, the manners, in which I may serve this purpose better.' and *mean* what is said, and *act* that way." (1436-1)

"Use that re-ionizer, the Radio-Active Appliance, as has been given. This revitalizes the system throughout!... Hence at such periods that the Appliance is used, we would use the same period for deep meditation. And as the Mind is the Builder, we will find that the revitalizing of the body will bring for the whole of the nervous system and also the whole regenerative system-new life, new energies awakened in same." (1472-2)

"And during such a period make this the time not for conversation but rather meditating upon the possibilities, the probabilities, upon the Infinite... Form for self a philosophy..." (949-5)

"Use the period when the Radio-Active Appliance is attached as a period not of conversation but rather of contemplation and meditation, as periods in which the body will review its own experiences in the earth, its relationships and what the body is planning to do with its life in relationships to others, and as to the reasons for the body being in the material experience in the present; and what it intends to do with the opportunities for being an expression of its ideals in this sojourn." (4030-1)

"Let the mental self meditate upon man and man's advent, his purposes, into the earth. Why and whence - and what for?" (1455-1)

"Become more acquainted with self, self's purposes, self's desires." (1893-1)

"It is the mental attitude now, that is to be corrected for the body. The body should be in this manner, as it were [literally], make a list of its beliefs, tenets, faiths, hopes and desires. Gradually, as these are studied, eliminate all that the body-mind sees are of a self-centered or selfish nature - the things it would like to do, associations - as to their purposes and the like. Such as this: If the body desires to labor or to employ its mind, Why? It is that there is to be rid of something? Or is it a constructive influence? Is it to be a selfish motive." (1467-13)

"With the Appliance and with the meditative forces that make for concentration, the body will be enabled to fit itself physically and mentally to be of greater service, to find more and greater opportunities for the expression of that gained..." (531-6)

The days when the Appliance is used "will be found to be, if it may be so termed, the 'lucky' days, or the periods when there is a closer association with the Creative Forces about the body." (1179-1)

"Use that hour as the period for definite meditation and prayer; not only for the removal of the disorders but that the purposes of the body and mind may be used for creative, constructive purposes - and not merely saying so." (3532-1)

"Let this be the period for prayer and meditation for the body to be used in the service for others, and not others in a service for the body. For the greater among men are those who serve the more." (4069-1)

"Read [Scriptures] not as history, read them not as axioms or as dogmas, but as of thine own being. For in the study of these ye will find that ye draw unto that force from which the writers of same gained their strength, their patience... He is the same yesterday, today and forever... to all is given according to the measure of their faith. And as ye apply this, though a mechanical implement made by man - yet also was the ephod, also was the altar made by man - yet these have brought, these may bring, these do bring, even the vision of the Cross, even as Gethsemane's Garden, even as the ordinance's have their place in the awakening of the consciousness of the inner being of a soul, of a man, so may this be not as a rosary, not as a picture, but rather as uniting the body, the mind, the soul with the Trinity - God, the Father, the Son, the Spirit. Thus may it bring to thee those experiences that are thine alone. And again He gives 'We have much work for thee to do!' " (1173-8)

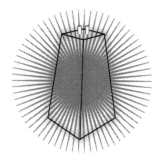

ARTICLES WRITTEN ABOUT THE RADIAC®

A Gift on the Doorstep
By Harvey Grady

A scientific study conducted on the RADIAC® "Impedance Device."

The Edgar Cayce medical readings repeatedly recommended a device that was supposed to be good for everyone's health - but it has been used by relatively few people. Until now no one knew exactly what it did to the body. And the U.S. Food and Drug Administration discouraged its sale and distribution because no scientific evidence of its benefits had been demonstrated.

The readings referred to it by several names: the Radial-Active Appliance; the Radial Machine; the Dry Cell; the Impedance Device; and the Radio-Active Appliance, which was the name most frequently used. But this last name led to some confusion after 1945 when the explosion of the first atomic bombs gave the term radioactivity an ominous connotation. Since the Cayce device had nothing to do with that kind of radioactivity, the Edgar Cayce Foundation suggested that a preferable name was the Impedance Device. Today it is known throughout the world as the RADIAC®. (pronounced RAY-DEE-ACK)

The Impedance Device was recommended in the readings for health maintenance and prevention of disease. It was said to be "good for anyone!" (826 - 3) "The vibrations from some are well for every human individual." (1800 - 15) Specifically, it was recommended for nervous tension and incoordination in 61 readings; circulatory incoordination (52); circulation (41); insomnia (35); neurasthenia (22); debilitation (16); hypertension(13); abnormal children (12); deafness (11); obesity (11); arthritis (11); and other conditions (170).

The readings suggest that it offers the advantage of correcting possible imbalances, equilibrating body energies, and attuning the vibrations of the body to an optimal state. It is said to stimulate the body and mind to better organize and integrate their functioning. It might improve memory and such other mental functions as clarification of purpose. It might also produce an altered state of consciousness similar to those achieved in meditation and creative visualization. Aerospace engineer James Beal has called it a "harmony generator".

Specifically, the readings indicated that the following beneficial physiological effects might be expected from using the device:

- Normalization of blood pressure
- Normalization of heart pulse rate
- Improvement in peripheral blood circulation
- Reduction in blood impurities
- Normalization of iron content in blood
- Normalization of electrolytes
- Normalization of kidney functions
- Normalization of oxygen content in blood
- Increase in blood coagulation capability
- Reduction in stress
- Improved sensory perception.

This list is based on only a superficial review of the medical readings, and a more comprehensive examination might expand the list of anticipated benefits. The extent of the effects would depend on the degree of the person's abnormal condition. If, for example, a person's blood pressure was very high, the device's effect would probably be greater than with a person having almost normal blood pressure.

The attitude of the user of the device is said to be a key factor in the results. A positive mental attitude, such as that associated with hope, faith, meditation, and prayer, was recommended. The readings warned against using it when one is in a negative mental or emotional state.

But what exactly is the Impedance Device?

It looks much like a battery, because it has two terminals - one terminal connected by a copper wire to a copper (positive) electrode, and the other terminal to a nickel (negative) electrode. The electrodes attach to the body - one to the wrist of one arm, the other to the ankle of the opposite side. But it is not a battery. It contains no electrical energy of its own, as a charged battery does. Instead, when attached as recommended, it utilizes the body's electrical currents.

Its electrical design appears to be that of a capacitor surrounded by a resistance. It is made of rectangular container that holds two parallel carbon-steel plates separated by two panes of glass, and surrounded by blocks of carbon and powdered charcoal. Its design creates a capacitor which theoretically modulates the current flowing from one part of the body to another. It puzzles conventional biomedical engineers because it would appear incapable of producing any physiological effect, since the body's electrical current would seem too weak to bridge the capacitor. But biomedical engineers familiar with the principals of acupuncture theorize that it serves to modulate the flow of body energy in some manner.

The readings describe the device as effecting a change in the electrical energies of the body. But just how it works remains a matter of conjecture. Stanford University physicist William Tiller theorizes that it balances the energy flow in the body through the acupuncture meridians known to Chinese medicine for perhaps 5,000 years. Professor Tiller speculates that the device may set up a gentle oscillating energy flow through the meridians, causing electric current to flow out of some acupuncture points and into others, at levels probably below one micro-ampere (one millionth of an ampere of current). Dr. William A. McGarey, who uses acupuncture in his medical practice, agrees with Tiller's speculation.

Other theories involve hypotheses of subtle energies related to radionics or orgone, which are not presently detectable by electromagnetic means. Although some of these theories are interesting, they are not currently testable. Scientific investigation of the device must utilize accepted physiological measurements and some newly developed electrical measurements of acupuncture meridians.

In an effort to determine the precise effects of the device, the Fetzer Energy Medicine Research Institute in 1987 launched a pilot study which included the first scientific double-blind experiment to ascertain what happens when a person uses the RADIAC®. The pilot study first included an electronic analysis of devices, followed by an experimental study of the physical effect on individuals. While not conclusive due to the small number of test subjects, the study did indicate that the device had a measurable effect on the human neuroendocrine system.

Ten healthy volunteers were used in the pilot study; five were randomly assigned to the experimental group, and five were randomly assigned to the control group. All 10 persons received four 30-minute treatments on four consecutive days. The experimental group was treated with real devices, and the control group was treated with devices that looked and weighed exactly the same as the real devices, yet contained none of the elements of the real devices. These experimental and control devices were used in order to rule out a possible placebo effect, which might be due to a person's positive expectations of treatment.

Neither the volunteers nor the medical staff knew which volunteers had been treated by experimental or control devices. Only the research director knew the code used to mark the bottoms of the devices, thereby fulfilling double-blind conditions. One of the volunteers in the control group dropped out of the study, due to difficulty in maintaining the requirement of fasting prior to testing. This left four persons in the control group.

Baseline values of blood and urine biochemistry were established in the first day before the start of treatment, and on the fourth day blood and urine samples were taken again. The study was based on a before-and-after treatment comparison of blood and urine biochemistry. To reduce extraneous variables which might affect test results, volunteers were asked to refrain from tobacco, alcohol, and caffeine on test days, and also to fast for at least six hours prior to testing.

To follow Cayce-recommended procedure, volunteers were asked to relax in a reclining position on a bed and encouraged to pray, meditate, and/or rest quietly during the 30- minute period of treatment. The devices were placed in direct sunlight for almost an hour prior to placement in waxed paper buckets of ice water, where they chilled for 30 minutes. The positive (red) electrode was attached to the body about three minutes prior to the attachment of the negative (black) electrode. This practice was followed each of the four days, in accord with the sequence for electrode placement on opposite wrists and ankles as recommended by the Cayce readings. The same device was always attached to the same person.

The biochemical data samples included a complete blood count, catecholamine and chem-zyme evaluation of 30 cc. of blood serum, and a urinalysis of 10 cc. of urine, collected before and after treatment. Specific data included 59 factors, 55 of which consisted of routine medical tests which can be considered rather insensitive indicators of change, and four indicators of catecholamine levels which can be considered as more sensitive indicator of change. These factors provided a wide range for testing physiological response to a minimal level of treatment.

SmithKline Bio-Science Laboratories performed an independent biochemical analysis of blood and urine samples. A gross statistical analysis, based on group means, was conducted with SPSS-X computer software. With the small number of human subjects, group mean methodology could detect only relatively strong physiological effects. This approach suited a pilot study with a limited budget. If no physiological change was detected in the pilot study, then further study of the Cayce Impedance Device would require greater strength of treatment, as determined by a greater number of treatments over a longer period of time.

What the pilot study data showed was a possible significant increase in the level of serum dopamine in the experimental group, as compared to the control group. (This finding was based on a single-tailed T test with the critical value at the .10 significance level.)

Dopamine is involved in the control of fine motor function and circulation in the body. It is one of the neurotransmitters called catecholamines, which are the body's chemicals mainly involved in the stress response, or "fight or flight" response to perception of threat. Neurotransmitters consist of molecules which regulate the electrical activity of nerves. Neurotransmitters can stimulate or inhibit the electrical firing of nerve cells.

Dopamine is considered the first catecholamine created from the metabolism of essential amino acids, and is associated with relaxation. As metabolism continues, dopamine is converted to norepinephrine and then to epinephrine, which are associated with stress reactions such as an increase in blood pressure.

An increase in the amount of dopamine in the blood stream, resulting from treatment by the Cayce Impedance Device, will be associated with relaxation, and may be evidence of greater coordination of the circulation which relate to stress reduction and normalization of blood circulation. Based on this tentative finding, we can speculate that the device would benefit persons with decreased function in motor control and blood circulation.

The statistical analysis of the pilot study offers a promising suggestion, if not conclusive evidence, that the Cayce Impedance Device actually performs as the Cayce readings suggest. More definitive study of the device is needed. FEMRI has designed a one-year study and is now awaiting funding of $97,000 to implement the study.

The proposed study will compare the effects of the Impedance Device and sham control devices on 40 healthy volunteers, between 20 and 50 years of age, with no history of cardiovascular, respiratory, or neurological problems. Each person will be assigned randomly to experimental or control groups, which will each include 20 persons. A double-blind protocol will be followed, in which treatment will be administered under laboratory conditions at the FEMRI lab. Each person will visit the lab for treatment and the same time of day, four days a week, for three consecutive weeks, thereby receiving a total of 12 treatments in three electrode rotation cycles. Thus, a greater amount of treatment will be likely to produce stronger effects.

These 40 subjects will be tested for a number of physiological indicators before, during, and after treatment. A comparison of scores between experimental and control groups will provide evidence for statistically significant findings.

Data will include blood tests and urinalysis, as was done for the pilot study, plus daily physiological monitoring of brainwaves, heartbeat, respiration, and peripheral blood flow. Acupuncture meridian data will be collected with a special instrument developed by FEMRI. In total, close to 100 physiological indicators will be measured for each person. In addition, a brief psychological questionnaire will be administered before and after treatment, identifying a person's perceptions about his health and symptomatology.

As the Cayce readings recommended more that 50 years ago, the Impedance Device needs to be scientifically tested before it can truly be made available to the public for health care. Like a gift left unclaimed on the doorstep, the device would become a resource for health maintenance as a body energy balancer and stress reducer, if it is properly researched first. Furthermore, the device could also be used to treat persons with decreased function in motor control and blood circulation.

However, further study, involving larger numbers of people and physiological parameter, is needed for substantive research findings.

Radio-Active Appliance
by Elaine Hruska

"Good for Everybody"

The name itself may deter some from using this remedy: "radio-active," yet that's how this appliance was named and described in the readings. The device has no connection whatsoever with radioactivity, which became a household word after the 1945 detonation of the first atomic bombs. Possibly in some way it is comparable to a radio wave because of a vibrational current between it and the user. The Edgar Cayce Foundation suggested the name Impedance Device. Today it is known as the RADIAC® and is sold through A.R.E.'s official worldwide supplier, Baar Products, Inc.

What does it do?

According to the readings, the RADIAC® effects a change in the body's electrical energy by utilizing the body's own current. It looks like a battery, but contains no electrical energy of its own, though it does emit a subtle force often detected by sensitive individuals. The two terminals on the top of the appliance are each connected by a wire to an electrode or disc that is attached to the body. "Its design," according to Harvey Grady's article "A Gift on the Doorstep," "creates a capacitor which theoretically modulates the current flowing from one part of the body to another." This equalizing effect was mentioned in several readings, one of which stated:

"The Radio-Active Appliance is good for anyone, and especially for those that tire or need an equalizing of the circulation; which is necessary for anyone that uses the brain a great deal—or that is unactive on the feet as much as is sufficient to keep the proper circulation." (826-3)

Another person asked how long it should be used and received this reply:

"Oh, from thirty minutes to all evening! This doesn't matter so much— the time—under such conditions; but this would be good for anyone, see? especially to rest tired business men, overtaxed ladies—there are a few! and such conditions as go to make up for the physical exertions of the body, where taxation mentally, or taxation physically. These would be the greater aids. This is Number One." (1800-16)

Using the RADIAC®

A four-sided figure shaped slightly like a pyramid, this device was mentioned in over 800 Cayce documents. An instruction booklet for its care, use, and storage is included with each purchase. The RADIAC® can be used as is (plain) or with a solution jar attached. Primarily it was recommended to improve circulation or to normalize the functioning of the nervous system, most often as a preventative rather than a curative measure.

Until one gets used to the procedure, it may seem daunting at first to hook it up, with its discs, wires, and loop straps. But within a short time, the task should become "second nature." The appliance is placed in the sun for about an hour between uses (cloudy days are OK) in order to hold the vibrations that over time build up within it. Twenty minutes before you hook up to it, put the device into a plastic, glass, or ceramic (nonmetal) container (about a gallon-size) and fill the basin with ice up to the red strip one-and-a-half inches from the top of the appliance, then add water to the same level. The ice and cold water help to "electronize" the device. While it's resting in this tub, you may clean the surfaces of the electrode discs by polishing them with a cloth, then sanding them lightly with emery paper. This removes the film built up from the body's vibrations and prevents short-circuiting. After twenty minutes, connect the red (positive) wire to the red jack on the appliance. Connect the black (negative) wire to the black jack, making sure that the discs do not touch each other. Then attach the red disc to your body, next the black disc (always starting with the positive).

These electrodes are placed directly on the skin, attached with Velcro to maintain a firm contact, but not too tight to inhibit circulation. With each application they are rotated sequentially over the pulse points on the ankle (inner, big toe side) and wrist (thumb side of hand). In using a solution jar, the placement is slightly different, and it's best to follow a specific reading in choosing the positions for the discs. Length of time was about thirty minutes, at least in the beginning. While connected to the device, maintain a relaxed, meditative state, pray, or listen to soothing, inspirational music. At the end of the time period, when disconnecting, reverse the order, removing first the black (negative) attachment from your body, then the red (positive). Then remove the black wire from the appliance, followed by the red wire.

It is important to rest and relax for about thirty minutes after use, avoiding any excessive physical or mental activity, in order to allow the good effects to continue. Then, keeping the black and red wires separated, clean and polish the discs as before, and store them separately. The device is removed from the ice container, placed in the sun, and then stored away from any metal objects. The solution jar, if used, is taken care of at this time. After completing the four-day sequence, you can leave it off for four days to a week, then resume the cycle again.

Benefits of the RADIAC®

Bringing a better balance to one's body seems to be the main function of this rather mysterious, plain looking device. A pilot study, the first scientific double-blind experiment to determine what happens to people using the appliance, was launched in 1987 by the Fetzer Energy Medicine Research Institute. Analysis of its results indicated in the experimental group a possible significant increase in the level of serum dopamine as compared to the control group. Dopamine, a neurotransmitter, is involved in fine motor function and circulation. An increase would be associated with relaxation, which may be related to greater coordination, reducing stress and normalizing blood circulation. Though further study is needed, this pilot study suggests that the device may perform as the readings state.

Several cautions are worth noting. This is beneficial to anyone properly used! It is harmful, improperly used. "You can't use the Radio-Active Appliance and be a good 'cusser' or 'swearer'—neither can you use it and be a good hater. For it will work as a boomerang to the whole of the nervous system if used in conjunction with such an attitude." (1844-2)

If your body is actually building the charge that will be disseminated by the appliance throughout your body, it would be important to be mindful of what you are creating. For this reason also you should be the sole user of your device.

It is not to be used on the same day you are taking alcoholic beverages. It is not to be stored in the refrigerator or on or near metal.

Relieving nervousness, promoting rest and sleep, normalizing weight, improving vision and hearing, and creating a better metabolism—these are all benefits promised in individuals' readings for those who choose to avail themselves of this unique and specialized instrument.

RADIAC® is a Registered Trademark of Baar Products, Inc.

A FAMILY AFFAIR
By Barbara Derrick, Ph.D.

Eileen and the RADIAC®

Eileen Auxier thought she was doomed. Alzheimer's disease had begun to wrap its tentacles around her life. She was on a slow descent into the pit of no return. At 51 years of age she was going to inherit early Alzheimer's from her father.

Eileen was fulfilling a dream when the Alzheimer's nightmare blasted into her reality. A fulfilling and productive part of her life was behind her. Her children were grown and her music had earned her a place in the hearts of the congregation where she served as choir director. Her years of teaching were now offering a new possibility for the future. With additional skills she could offer kindergarten-age children special programs to enrich their lives. She wanted their hearts to sing, just as hers had done all her life.

The symphony of her life was about to stop when Eileen enrolled in a master's degree program in Music Pedagogy for preschool children and reality struck a discordant note. In class she would listen to the instructions, start to take notes, and the information would disappear. Unlike forgetting and thinking about it later, it was gone.

What must she do? She was not about to renege on her commitment to get the Master's degree. In order to get the degree she had to retain information given in class. Since she couldn't take notes, she used a tape recorder. She could replay the lecture many times.

The tape recorder satisfied the immediate need, but she knew she must devise another way to deal with the inevitable Alzheimer's. Medical science offered no help, but having been a student of Edgar Cayce for years (she was the first woman to hold the office of Chair of the A.R.E. Board of Trustees), she knew about the RADIAC® – the six-inch, royal blue pyramid with its flat top where two one-inch cylinders could be attached to its power source.

"I told my older Gunter brothers and sisters about it," Eileen said. "Through the years I tried to acquaint them with Cayce, but they weren't interested in Cayce or alternative medicine. The medical doctors enrolled them in research projects. When my siblings asked the doctors about Cayce and the RADIAC® they replied, 'There's nothing to it.'"

The Gunter family's illnesses were distressing. Eileen watched them fall, one by one, to the inevitable Alzheimer's. Her parents had eight children. From one parent, their father, they inherited early-onset Alzheimer's, and the late-onset form from their mother.

Indiana University wanted to research the family in which both parents carried early- and late-onset Alzheimer's genes. Blood samples were taken from all the family members who would allow it. Autopsies followed when death occurred if the "Family of Procreation" allowed it. Today, of the original 10 family members only Eileen and her younger brother, a retired United Methodist minister, survive. Their story is worth repeating.

Eileen watched her brothers and sisters travel a road toward the same destination. Her oldest sister, a second mom to her, died four years ago. When Eileen was six and entering the first grade, her sister was enrolling as a freshman in college. Eileen visited her sister often during her illness; one way Eileen could show her devotion.

Aricept, a recently developed drug for treatment of Alzheimer's, helped her sister, but before she got its temporary reprieve, her sister hid her agony from her husband. She told Eileen she could cry buckets, but didn't want to do that to her husband.

"I could see the Alzheimer's look in her eyes," Eileen recalls. After she moved to assisted living, her sister would forget when Eileen was coming and was surprised when she came to visit.

With the Aricept she could understand a lot of words. She could laugh but not communicate. The Alzheimer's had robbed her of that skill. She could say only a word or two, or a sentence once in a while. The drug enabled her to sit with her husband and watch television, but it quit working after a period of time and she deteriorated. She did not live as long as her mother, who had no treatment whatsoever.

Eileen's mother showed unmistakable signs of Alzheimer's at 72. By her early 80s she had to be placed in an assisted-living home. The family could not provide the care they knew she needed. She no longer recognized her loved ones. In a nursing home she slept away most of her last 10 years.

Indiana University recorded as much as they could. Eileen's father had early onset and although he died of a heart attack at 70, he had labored with Alzheimer's for 15 years before his death. The man who loved to read and could remember measurements in his carpentry work, became one who no longer read and had to repeat again and again the measurements he had just taken.

Eileen started regular daily sessions with the RADIAC®. She attached one electrode to one arm and the second to the opposite ankle, moving the electrodes around her body clockwise on consecutive nights. She was in no hurry. The readings say, "Be patient. You must be patient." Patient meant months and years, not days and weeks.

"I didn't start my RADIAC® until about age 60. I was busy and this was an annoyance," Eileen recalls. "But I started the RADIAC®, because I knew that by 70 I'd be in bad shape otherwise. I was traveling, and teaching for Kindermusic International. I couldn't take the Wet Cell since the Wet Cell can't be moved. The RADIAC® can be moved. The only restriction on the use of the RADIAC® was that it must be placed in the sun every day. I was strong and healthy and the RADIAC® suited me because it used my own energy. The Wet Cell generates an imperceptible but measurable amount of power and is stronger. Ed Rocks described the Wet Cell as the RADIAC® on steroids."

Then came another disappointment. Eileen heard her younger brother Doyce search for a word. He could not remember the exact word he wanted. Eileen had experienced the same frustration herself. He tried to disguise his inability to retrieve the word by beginning the sentence again and substituting another word for the one that eluded him. Eileen's heart crumbled. Her family history to date was dismal:

- Her father had early onset, obvious in his 50s. He died at age 70.
- Her mother had later-life onset, obvious in her late 60s. She died at age 90.
- Two sisters and one brother had early onset. They died at age 57, 64, and 67, respectively.
- One sister and one brother had later-life onset. Both died at 84.

Eileen has used the Baar RADIAC® for 12 years to prevent Alzheimer's. Two years after starting treatment she regained full memory capacity and is not showing any signs of Alzheimer's at the present time.

When Eileen recognized Doyce's symptoms she told him, "You know that our siblings followed the research route. I plan to use the RADIAC®. You can do what you wish." He replied, "I'm going to do what you do, sis."

Doyce started using the RADIAC® at age 60, the same age that Eileen began. He was faithful to the sessions, taking them regularly and being sure to think positive and faith-filled thoughts when he was attached to the RADIAC®.

He is now living in Tupelo, Mississippi, enjoying life after retirement from a 50-year ministry in the Methodist church.

Both appliances, then, were suited to the Auxiers. David needed the stronger infusion of power while Eileen and her brother Doyce Gunter profited from the RADIAC®, which redistributed their own energy.

Today Eileen and Doyce are the only two surviving members of the Gunter family and the only two to follow Edgar Cayce's advice. Eileen, Dave, and Doyce are doing well and plan to continue using the Edgar Cayce appliances that have served them so well.

Edited from Venture Inward Magazine May/June 2006 Issue.

My Experience with Lyme's Disease & The RADIAC®
by W. Greenwald

Over a five year period I was treated seven times for Lyme's disease. It started with a tick bite in June 1999. I removed the tick and monitored the site for a rash or "bull's eye", typical of Lyme's infections. There was no skin reaction so I believed that I was not infected. Later, I was to learn that less than 30% of infected people ever develop a rash. About 8 weeks after the bite I had severe headaches and by 9 weeks heart palpitations started. That got my serious attention. The blood test available at that time indicated that I was not infected, but urine test results confirmed that I was "in the mid to later stages of infection". Almost at the same time, my wife, Marge, was bitten, infected and developed a skin reaction. A program of antibiotics cured her in short order and she has been fine since. Seems that if you get it early that a cure is easy. A standard treatment of antibiotics cured me of all my symptoms.

At that time, no test could tell if you had been cured. I was bitten again and symptoms returned. At that time, no test could determine if you were newly infected or had been infected some time in the past. Currently, a DNA blood test can tell which of about 11 tick borne diseases you have. "Markers" or "Bands" appear in the test results.

The combination of markers is like a finger print and identifies which disease is present. During those five years, the DNA test once showed that I was free of Lyme's, but had a tick disease similar to Malaria. Anti-Malarial medication worked fine. Each time I had Lyme's symptoms, a stronger and/or different drug or drug combination was used until the symptoms stopped. I have no evidence that I was bitten more than twice, but the disease "flared up" again and again.

Medical opinion became that the spirochetes causing the Lyme's would "hide" in deep muscle or possibly bone and emerge later to cause a new infection called a "flare up". Each treatment took longer until I was symptom free, but I believe, never truly free of the spirochetes.

My last infection was treated with 500mg of Zithromax EVERY day for seven months plus a weekly injection of Penicillin. Zithromax is a very strong antibiotic and normally three days of use will cure most infections for which it is used.

It was during this last infection that my wife, who is a nurse, thought that I had reached a plateau. We agreed that I was not getting better. For the first time, I searched the web for information concerning Lyme's. No one had found a cure or even gave any hope of help for long term infections.

The next step came because of my long term use and understanding of the RADIAC®. I have used a RADIAC® unit for many years either by itself or with a solution in a jar. I thought that if silver injections could kill Syphilis spirochetes, then maybe the vibrations of silver could do the same for Lyme's spirochetes. The spirochetes might try to hide, but they could not escape the silver vibrations that would flow through every part of my body. I knew from experience that I ALWAYS felt better after using the #155 Gold Solution with the RADIAC®.

In mid March, 2004, I got #185 Baar Compound Solution from Baar Products, Inc. (610-873-4591 or their web page is www.baar.com) and started the four day (30 minutes per day) cycle around my body. After two days into the cycle, I started to feel worse. That was actually good news. I knew from experience that what my doctor had said was true. When spirochetes die they produce toxins that can make you feel very poorly. I completed the 4 day cycle. For 2 more days after the cycle I felt badly. Then I slowly started to feel better.

About two weeks after this cycle, I decided to repeat it. This time I did not get a toxins reaction so I believed that all the spirochetes might be dead. To be certain, I repeated the 4 day cycle with fresh silver in early April. Again, no toxins response. By the end of April my doctor agreed that I could stop taking the Zithromax and Penicillin. I started to feel even better. It has been 9 months since that first cycle and I have no Lyme's symptoms. My energy level and endurance have returned to normal. Should I become bitten and infected again my first response will be to use the RADIAC® with the silver.

Here, in Chester County, PA, there were 903 confirmed cases of Lyme's disease in 2003. It is not a trivial disease for long term patients. There are about 50 different symptoms. My doctor also had the disease, so he was very aware of the problems I was facing which were severe headaches, heart palpitations, extreme fatigue, poor sleep patterns, no dreams, falling asleep during the daytime, short term memory loss (that was scary!), and continual depression without a desire to do anything. I am SO thankful to report that all these symptoms are gone!!! Hopefully, other long term

Lyme's patients will receive help from the RADIAC®, as I did.

In August and again in September 2004, medical science proved twice, by a series of blood tests, that I am FREE of Lyme's Disease.

Healing the Energy Body
By Len Kasten

The Cayce Appliance Rediscovered

The Medicine of the 21st Century

Now, with the 21st Century almost upon us, it is becoming increasingly clear to many of those in the alternative health movement, both practitioners and patients, that good health is not obtained by simply treating physical cells and organs. More and more, as they observe the startling results of certain holistic practices, they are coming to the inescapable conclusion that freedom from disease, and vibrant good health has more to do with that aspect of the body that is apparently bio-electric and invisible, which is to say - non-physical. More recently it has been referred to as the "bioplasmic," or "energy" body. Alternative healing techniques such as acupuncture, yoga, polarity therapy, hypnotherapy, psychic healing, and other modalities, manipulate the energy flow in this body, which appears to improve physical health dramatically. It has also been noticed that positive mental states (Bernie Siegal, Deepak Chopra, Bill Moyers, et al), even humor (Norman Cousins) have a beneficial effect on health. The "mind," in this context, is clearly not the physical brain, but rather something that *uses* the brain. This suggests that it would probably be the bio-electric counterpart of the brain. Furthermore, thanks to Kirlian photography, this bio-electric body can actually be seen, and relative health can be diagnosed by the colors and vibrancy showing up on the Kirlian photograph. So, they have come to conclude, therefore, that the medicine of the 21st Century will expand and improve on these techniques, and will focus primarily on the bioplasmic body and on mind-body reciprocal influences.

The Electrical Body

Freud was the first to propose the existence of something called "psychic energy," which he named the "libido," a concept that the hardheaded scientific physicians of his time found to be laughable. Then, the Theosophists spoke of the "seven bodies of Man." But it was Edgar Cayce who took the matter out of the realm of psychological and metaphysical speculation, and brought it right down to practical application. Cayce was full of surprises. In the voluminous pages of health-related Cayce readings at the A.R.E are many strange remedies, most of which were never heard of before he spoke of them, e.g. animated ash, and atomic iodine. But strangest of all are the "Rube Goldberg" appliances that he recommended for a wide array of ailments from mild arthritis all the way up to neurological disease, and even cancer. He mentions these devices in over 1,000 of the health readings, and gives very specific instructions for constructing two different models. They appear to be some sort of batteries capable of accumulating and/or boosting an extremely low electrical charge. Cayce says that these devices tap the body's inherent electrical energy, change it, and then feed it back. He claims that the physical body is suffused with electricity, which he claims to be identical with the "life force." He says, "the lowest form of electrical vibration is the basis of life," and "all energy is electrical in its activity in a manifested form." This is basically heresy as far as the medical model is concerned. He is taking the position that what we refer to as physical energy does not come from the consumption and oxidation of food, but rather from an external source. The body's electrical pulsations are, he says, "the lowest form of electrical forces that move as energies from the etheronic forces.... or the electrical creative forces." To translate loosely and taking some liberties, he is saying here that the bio-electric body gives life by acting as the intermediary between the life force and the physical body. Conversely, we can reasonably conclude that when it departs, the life force departs, and that is what we call death.

The RADIAC®, Radio-Active Appliance

From the teachings of acupuncture practitioners, we learn that the bioplasmic body is a highly complex etheric organism, laced with hundreds of meridians and dotted with 700 energy focal points. From other Eastern sources we learn that it is highly differentiated and has seven major energy centers called the chakras. The structure and organization of the physical body corresponds to the differentiation of the bioplasmic body. Consequently each part of the physical body has a different electrical vibratory rate based on its bioplasmic counterpart. Cayce puts it this way, "the human body (is) made up of electronic vibration, with each atom and element of the body, each organ and organism of same, having its... unit of vibration necessary for the sustenance of, and equilibrium in, that particular organism...When any force in any organism...becomes deficient in its ability to reproduce that (electrical) equilibrium necessary for the sustenance of...physical existence, that portion becomes deficient ...through (in) electronic energy..." To redistribute the "electronic" energy, taking it from a part of the body where there is a surplus, and supplying it to a deficient part, he recommended the Radial Active Appliance. The unit is immersed in ice water contained in a non-metallic bucket, and, when the temperature has cooled sufficiently, i.e. after about 30 minutes, wires from each pole with plates on the ends are placed on the body. The placement was carefully spelled out by Cayce. One lead goes on the pulse point of the right wrist, and the other on the left ankle. (It should be noted that these are acupuncture points). Then they are rotated to the four different wrist-ankle combinations from day to day. Cayce suggested this device as a sort of general tonic. He says, "It will be found to aid the body in every direction," and "The Radio-Active Appliance is good for anyone, and especially for those that tire or need an equlibrizing of the circulation." His claims for this appliance sometimes border on the extravagant - "...it may keep its body in almost perfect accord for many - many - many - many - many days." And in another reading, "...a type of appliance for bringing rest to the weary, rest to those who have been inclined to depend on sedatives, and narcotics for rest; to those who have been under great periods of stress and strain... ."

The device directly affects the nervous system, but by balancing and rejuvenating the neurological network, it also improves those systems most affected by the nerves, i.e. the circulation and the endocrine system. As the circulation becomes more normalized, the blood pressure decreases. It also sharpens all the senses. He says, "...for even those of the sensory system - in eyes, keenness of taste, keenness of hearing - will respond to these." Perhaps the most interesting advice given by Cayce in conjunction with this appliance is the recommendation that the time of its use, about an hour each day, be used also for prayer and meditation, expressing good expectations, and inner reverence and sincerity. This will have the effect, he says, of "making a better coordination between all...mental and spiritual and physical forces," thus increasing the efficacy of the session. Conversely, if the attitude is impatient, and the thoughts are negative, he says, it could have no effect, and could even boomerang and damage the nervous system (361-8). Thus, Cayce emerges as one of the earliest advocates in the U.S. of the mind-body influences.

The Wet Cell

While the Radio-Active Appliance is effective for general health improvement, for those with serious problems, Cayce rolled out the heavy artillery - the Wet Cell Appliance. This device is similar, but uses different materials, and doesn't require immersion in ice water. The plate on the wire from the positive copper pole is first placed on the spine at various points in the dorsal (now thoracic) region. The wire from the negative nickel pole is passed via a metal loop through another solution before being placed on the body. This solution normally is gold chloride (1-2 grains to one ounce of distilled water), but could also be Spirits of Camphor or Nitrate of Silver, depending on the person and the specific ailment. This plate is placed on the solar plexus, just above the navel.

Unlike the Radio-Active device, the Wet Cell does produce a minute voltage. Apparently, the electrical vibrations of whatever substance is used, are added to the boosted electrical charge being fed back into the body via the negative pole, at the solar plexus, each solution type affecting the body differently. The Gold Chloride primarily affects the circulation, whereas the Silver Nitrate works on the endocrine system, but both impact the nervous system. Cayce recommended that the gold and silver solutions be used on alternate days. The Spirits of Camphor, he claimed, aided the digestive and lymphatic systems. Sometimes, for thyroid-related problems, he recommended a solution of his electrically charged iodine, called Atomic Iodine.

Cayce recommended the Wet Cell for some serious ailments, and made some spectacular claims for its capabilities. He said that it was much more powerful than the Radio-Active device. The list of conditions that he maintained would be helped by the Wet Cell is very long and all-encompassing. It includes many debilities that would appear to have no connection with the nervous system, such as both hypotension and hypertension, anemia, rheumatism, tuberculosis, diabetes, venereal disease, and even kidney stones! But nervous disorders, such as Cerebral Palsy, MS, Parkinson's Disease, epilepsy, vertigo, et al are prime candidates for Wet Cell treatments. In one of the most interesting readings about the Wet Cell (466-1), Cayce claimed that this device can actually reverse senility! He says, "...with the proper manipulations to produce coordination... as may be given...osteopathically, or neuropathically...*may create for a body almost a new brain.*"! (exclamation point is the author's). In other words, this device rejuvenates the nervous system at a cellular level. Consequently, it achieves the most obvious results in all cases of degenerative disease.

The Wet Cell is a sort of a fountain of youth, capable of returning the entire body to a young, flexible condition by repairing lapses in the nerve complexes, the effects of which cascade throughout the system. Apparently it restores the proper vibratory pattern for nerve cell reproduction, which sometimes deteriorates, frequently, but not necessarily, with age. Deterioration of the bioplasmic body evidently can result from a variety of mental-spiritual pathologies, regardless of age, which somehow shut off "the healer within." For this reason, Cayce always stressed the fact that the device alone, without a mental-spiritual transformation, could only be a temporary palliative. Just as with the RADIAC device, he urged a spiritual reverence, and a positive mental attitude while using the appliance. He also recommended some associated therapies, primarily massage or osteopathic manipulation, and dietary improvement, comprising a complete recovery program.

Atlantean Medicine

The original devices were built for Edgar Cayce, while he was alive, by a man named Gray Salter, and then Marston Godfrey. Then, in the mid Fifties, after Cayce and Godfrey had passed away, Lester Babcoke, who also lived in Virginia Beach, inherited the mantle and was endorsed by the A.R.E. Babcoke was an electrical engineer, but was apparently deeply into metaphysics and the Cayce readings, and was something of an eccentric. He built thousands of the Radial-Active devices and the Wet Cells in his garage for over 25 years, and was basically the sole supplier until his death in 1982. At that point, the A.R.E. selected Bruce Baar to take over production. Baar, a Pennsylvanian, who had worked for Johnson & Johnson for many years, and a lifelong researcher of the Cayce readings, bought up all of Babcoke's materials and apparatus. He told us that he had allergies and asthma as a child, and had restored his health by extracting advice from the readings. Bruce Baar has since expanded his operation, and his company, Baar Products Inc., is now international, offering many of the other Cayce remedies as well as adjunctive health products. The Baar appliances are sold in the A.R.E. bookstore, and can also be purchased through his company website www.baar.com.

Testimonials

While the A.R.E. does not publish results or statistics of successes or failures of these devices, there are several "flagship" cases that have become notorious in recent years. David Atkinson, from Salisbury, North Carolina, is probably the most striking case of apparent remission from the dreadful Lou Gehrig's disease, or amyotrophic lateral sclerosis (ALS). Once contracted, this syndrome relentlessly destroys the nervous system, step by step, resulting in eventual paralysis of the motor system, and inevitably the patient dies within a short period of time when the involuntary motor functions cease. Atkinson, a former athlete, was diagnosed with the MNO (Motor Neuron Disease) variation of ALS in the Spring of 1991 at the age of 55, and he also displayed the tremors symptomatic of Parkinson's disease. The prognosis was continued deterioration, and an early death. Then, through his daughter, Atkinson was introduced to the A.R.E. and the Cayce readings. He traveled to Virginia Beach, and he read the only reading on ALS, 5019-1. Having been more or less atheistic, he immediately embarked on a spiritual renewal program of prayer and bible reading, and he followed the Cayce recipe for ALS recovery to the letter. He acquired a Baar Wet Cell, and used it every day, arranged to get daily massages, and took the recommended gold sodium and bromide of soda solutions. He also changed his diet. Atkinson is now, seven years later, much stronger, and physically active. Clearly, he has cheated death. Bruce Baar has several pages of other testimonials for both devices.

Clearly, the age of "energy medicine" has arrived, thanks to Edgar Cayce, and the future possibilities are spectacular. Many researchers believe that nerve regeneration will become commonplace, and just like the salamander, we will eventually be able to re-grow amputated limbs. But even more exciting, as we learn more about the bio-electric body, we will begin to really understand the nature of life and death, and that, in turn will lead inevitably to a spiritual renaissance for the entire human race.

For more information about the Cayce appliances contact:
Baar Products, Inc.
P.O. Box 60
Downingtown, PA 19335
1-800-269-2502 or 610-873-4591
www.baar.com

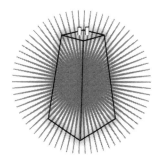

PRESENT DAY RADIAC® TESTIMONIALS

We thought it would be important to you to hear from every day users of the ***RADIAC®.*** *In the following section you will discover the heartfelt messages and personal experiences of people whose lives have been positively affected through use of the* ***RADIAC®.*** *Keep in mind, everyone's experience is different and may not be as noticeable in the short term as some of these.*

"I have enjoyed using my **RADIAC** unit. I have found that it has really helped with the neuropathic flares that I was getting in my fingers and toes. They have nearly disappeared. I am also enjoying better, more restful sleep." *L.C., West Lafayette, IN*

"The **RADIAC** is Built Excellently - Two Thumbs Up!" *D.C., Canada*

"I am sending you comments about my experiences upon using my personal **RADIAC**. The first time that I used my **RADIAC**; I did not expect to feel any different as the directions that came included with my **RADIAC** indicated that most people do not feel any noticeable changes...I was very pleasantly surprised after my first use...as I felt very peaceful, relaxed, and much more focused and at ease that lasted on into the evening. I thought to myself, 'I didn't realize what I was missing previously." *S.M., Ashville, NC*

"I recently received my **RADIAC** starter kit. All I can say is WOW! I will continue to update in the future. Thank you." *D.J., Bourbonnias, IL*

"I received the **RADIAC**, Hooray! I used it last night, and I felt some very strong action!" *T.R., Hauppauge, NY*

"My son is getting amazing results with the **RADIAC**. His occupational therapists say he performed amazingly yesterday with his speech and motion." *K.D., Stamford, CT*

"I celebrated my 76th birthday last Christmas. In early January I came down with sciatica in my right leg. My acupuncturist was not making good results. I couldn't sleep at night—was exhausted —and the pain was so intense it was weakening my heart. I couldn't take it anymore. I fell three times in my home, and held onto the walls whenever I walked in the home. I realized the acupuncturist was not helping. I cancelled my appointments with her....and turned to the **RADIAC**. With one treatment, pain was gone! Miracle of Miracles. I am continuing my treatments with the **RADIAC**. God Bless You." *E. G., Deerfield, IL.*

"I'm really excited about using the **RADIAC**. I've already lost my craving for sugar. Thank you, Edgar Cayce and Bruce Baar!" *K.M., CA*

"The **RADIAC** is a wonderful product from Baar! It has enhanced my life in so many ways! I dream deeper & my dreams are vivid! I feel as though I have so much more energy than I did prior to owning my **RADIAC**! Thank you so much Baar!" *D.S., Burlington, NC*

"I suffer from Lyme disease and planned to live a very depressed, confused, and painful life. I used the **RADIAC** and [Vibradex®] Solution #185. I have found the solution to be more effective than a long-course of doxicyclene antibiotics. This solution has taken me from living with about 50% of my normal vitality before Lyme disease to about 95% of my normal vitality. Without this solution, I would be hopeless. One four day treatment with this solution was more powerful than the doxcicyclene. Baar's Solution #185 is saving my life." *N.S., Afton, VA*

"Since I have started using the **RADIAC** I have been sleeping much more soundly. It feels great to wake up feeling totally rested. My energy level has gone up, too. I look forward to starting the day with more pep and vigor. Not only am I feeling much better, but my meditations are much better!" *E.W., Bellevue, WA*

"I believe the **RADIAC** helped me to retain a youthful appearance, have more strength and energy, reduce stress in my life, and get the rest and sleep I need." *D.D., Hampton, VA*

"I find meditating and relaxing are much more enjoyable somehow when connected to the **RADIAC**." *A.D., Allen Park, MI*

"During the time which I was using the **RADIAC** I felt a sensation of energy flow, particularly in my right arm. I also became very relaxed while lying on the floor, which is not normally a surface on which I could relax easily. Subsequently, I have used the appliance three times. The primary result to date while using the appliance appears to be enhanced relaxation." *D.B., Chicago, IL*

"I have used the **RADIAC** for a long time. It brings me more rest, and more mental and physical coordination than anything I ever tried - my whole body becomes stronger from using it." *B.J., Los Angeles, CA*

"[After using the **RADIAC**] I had vivid, pleasant dreams. I began to feel more relaxed and at ease than I had in a long time. I got stronger and gained weight, was able to return to work and completely regained my health. I'm literally reaching stages of health and well being that I have not previously experienced!" *R.R., Seattle, WA*

"I suspect the **RADIAC** has improved my metabolism. I have lost a few pounds since I started. I have been exercising more and eating healthier, but it seems like the weight is coming off easier than ever." *L.J., Cherry Hill, NJ*

"I have had wonderful success with helping me feel more energized & more well balanced sense of well being. This appliance [**RADIAC**] has had a very positive effect on my life." *D.D., Chicago, IL*

"The **RADIAC** system is an excellent product of high quality. I use the unit regularly with significant results." *A.J., Virginia Beach, VA*

"It [**RADIAC**] helps my circulation and makes me feel better." *W.L., Lakeland, FL*

"My overall impression was that of a general sense of well-being, along with a happy and light-hearted disposition that I seemed to have lost over the past several months. With regular use of the **RADIAC**...I've noticed a dramatic decrease in negative thoughts and an increase in energy." *D.C.*

"During the past 4 or 5 years, I have been using the **RADIAC** regularly and find that it has helped me maintain a level of energy, excitement and concentration that is very satisfying to me and apparently amazes my much younger associates. I am 80 years old and still working full time." *H.F., Lake Bluff, IL*

"I had been suffering from chronic fatigue and insomnia for years. Since using the **RADIAC** these problems have disappeared. It has made it possible for me to live a normal life. I found that it also helped me to lose weight when I went on a diet. It kept my energy level up and I was able to stick to my diet. ...I have not regained the weight I lost." *E.S., GA*

"When I was approximately 45 years old I was suffering with a lower back problem which had been progressively worsening for a year or more during which time I was visiting an osteopath regularly to no avail. It was at that time that I found the **RADIAC** appliance and I ordered one immediately. After using it for eight nights... I was running and playing with neighborhood children. Another problem was a torn ligament below the elbow which prevented the use of the two fingers. After a four night cycle I regained use and was back to normal... It improves my complexion and gives me energy and a feeling of well being. In my opinion it has very fine regenerative capabilities." *F.M., Richmond, VA*

"I ordered a **RADIAC** device from Bruce Baar. Almost immediately, I sensed a change from the pushed, shaky feelings I'd been having. The readings say this heightens all the senses, including memory. Specifically, sight, hearing, and taste are improved." *D.L., NJ*

"I mainly was interested in this appliance as a preventative measure, but the wonder of it all came when I found it to sweeten and soften the edge around every aspect of my life. I did have the problem of a short fuse with menopause symptoms due to low estrogen. Even that has changed…I take extra care with keeping the plates clean and my appliance gets a big dose of sunshine everyday. Again, it such a blessing from God to receive this boost. Thank you so much." *C.S., SC*

"I was unable to write for the last two months and after starting the **RADIAC**, alternating use of [Vibradex® Solutions] Gold and Silver, I was once again able to write. The arthritic pain in my hip has also reduced considerably." *R.S., NY*

"I have a stressful occupation and without the **RADIAC** to reduce my stress each evening and give me healthier, more peaceful sleep, I would probably find it most difficult to continue at my hectic pace. …does everyone who uses it feel and look younger?" *S.B., San Diego, CA*

"I have used my **RADIAC** 14 times now and always feel some current in my body, which feels similar to the energies felt after Yoga practice. Thank you for this product. This is a real magical experience for me." *J.O., Iceland*

"I have been using the **RADIAC** on and off since September, 1995. I found that it does help me to relax more during meditation…My body gets warm after maybe 20 minutes of usage during my 30 minute meditation." *A.C., Reno, NV*

"I once told my husband that if I had to make one choice and give up everything else, that choice would be my **RADIAC**! I use it almost every day. I sleep beautifully and stay healthy though I'm almost 75 and take no medications!" *H.N., Valley Center, CA*

"How I wish I had started to use this appliance [**RADIAC**] years ago. At once, I felt a flow of energy on my entire left side. This has now changed as I feel energy flowing throughout my entire body. My sleep certainly is deeper, and with less waking up in the middle of the night. I have vivid dreams and can recall them easier. My meditations also are deeper and the kundalini is flowing. I have a calmer attitude of all that would normally disturb my peace. It seems as if I could go on and on for I believe - no - I know that whatever this appliance does - it has made all areas of my life (spiritual, physical, and mental) better." *E.R.L., Sharon, PA*

"The **RADIAC** has already helped me calm down and feel more centered after only three applications!" *M. N., Milwaukee, WI*

"I have the **RADIAC**, my mother has one, and my sister got it last Friday to England. I like it very much; it gives quite immediately a feeling of height and a powerful pulsation especially in my chest, though it is very easy to meditate at the same time. My feet are really warm. My mother's health has been bad for many years – she has difficulties with balance. She has been inside all the time. This week she has been outside three times. She has used **RADIAC** over a month every day." *I.N., Finland*

"The **RADIAC** has helped me to sleep better and be calmer. This has especially been proven to me by my health practitioners who take my pulse. Thanks for making such a good product." *W.F., Pacific Palisades, CA*

"The **RADIAC** is for real! I have used it on and off for about three years now…When used in the evening or nighttime on a regular basis, I find it helps me feel more mentally focused, calm and collected during the day." *S. S., Maderson, SD*

"I have used the **RADIAC** four times - one cycle- and I love it. I felt it changing my energy from the first use. The night after using it, I sleep so much more peacefully. I also have had more vivid dreams. If I'd known how useful it is, I would have purchased one a long time ago." *N. G., Rutland, VT*

"About four and a half years ago I purchased a Baar **RADIAC**. Immediately, I began using the **RADIAC** on a daily basis. After approximately three weeks of use, my blood pressure dropped. My blood pressure is currently 120/80. I continue to use the **RADIAC** and have been very happy with its quality. For the last two years I have used my **RADIAC** with a [Vibradex®] Gold Solution. I would recommend the Baar **RADIAC** without reservation to anyone. I have purchased four additional Baar **RADIAC**s since my first, giving them as gifts to family members and friends. It has been far and away the most valuable physical treatment I have found." *J.M., Fairfax, Virginia*

"I've been using the **RADIAC** every day for about two months now and would recommend it to anyone. I feel great. I have more energy and my spirits have improved. My body 'tingles' with healing energy all day long. I feel GREAT! Today I recommended the **RADIAC** to one of my friends. Thank you for making the **RADIAC**. I appreciate that your device enhances my life!" *L. F., Lawndale, CA*

"I've used my **RADIAC** about 11 times now, and I find that I sleep more deeply, dream more vividly and recuperate from colds more quickly when using it!" *T.B., Laurel Hill, FL*

"Wonderful experience. I am now completely calm – no nervous tension. I can once again sleep throughout the night. I am more coordinated with a much better sense of balance. The overall effect is nothing short of miraculous. It is so wonderful to be able to sit and relax without being agitated." *J. O., San Leandro, CA*

"I've used the **RADIAC** off and on for several months. I sleep better, less tossing and turning and require less sleep. I feel more calm and relaxed and I believe I interact with others with a more constructive attitude!" *D.H., Northfield, MN*

"I sleep much deeper and dream more, and I feel more attuned with my Higher Self. The pulsing energy washes through imbalances in my nervous system and feels like it's freeing me. This device, as mysterious as it seems, is for real, and exactly what Cayce said it was." *J. M., Minn., MN.*

"After using my **RADIAC** for 16 days, I am happy to inform you that the results are amazing. Before, I was always so tired in the evening and no energy to do nice things. Now I feel great again. I am enjoying my life again. My health has much improved. My age is 55 years old. Before using the **RADIAC**, I really felt old. Now I am very busy again and happy that terrible, sleepy feeling is gone completely. Many thanks to the provider of the **RADIAC**! Kind Regards." *S. C., Gravenhage, Netherlands*

"The **RADIAC** is quite the little gizmo. Not to sound like a broken record, but I experienced the same thing as in the testimonials. Better circulation from the knees down, better eliminations, more energy, better attitude, more focused, my internal time clock and concentration is much better. The best part is what it did for my muscles in my neck, shoulders and arms. It took a few rounds, but every time it gets better. I would recommend this device to anyone; I was so impressed with it, I bought one for my wife." *S.T., Sioux Falls, ID*

"The **RADIAC** with the [Vibradex®] Gold Solution is amazing! The first night I used it I had a dream which solved a lifelong personal problem. The third night, I had a dream which helped solve a medical problem. It has also tremendously helped my energy and memory. This is a God send! Thank you." *C.B., Encinitas, CA*

"Before I received my **RADIAC**, I had often felt low energy levels in the afternoon as well as a frequent lack of ambition. Within the first couple of weeks, I realized that those feelings were mostly gone, and the increase in my overall energy has been consistent, along with a general feeling of well-being... Another surprise benefit has been improvement in my eyesight. I have used cheap reading glasses as needed for about the past 15-20 years. A few weeks ago I realized that I no longer require them when working on the computer and for some of my reading." *G.M., Downey, CA*

"I have been using the **RADIAC** now for over six months. Having been initiated into a number of spiritual practices over the years including Kriya and Sant Mat, I can honestly say I have found nothing more powerful than using the **RADIAC** for meditation. It has so far been an extraordinary journey. Many things have changed on the physical level: I am far more creative (which is good, because I am an artist!). I have a great deal more energy- exercising at least five times per week from barely at all. My circulation and digestion have greatly improved, as has the flexibility of both my mind and body. I sleep far better and in general my consciousness remains in a positive frame, even in situations where I would have previously been knocked off balance. I am also beginning to look and feel much younger. And last, but by no means least, Bruce Baar has been extremely helpful in answering any questions along the way. I am very grateful." *G.C., Ojai, CA*

"The **RADIAC** gives me a very, cozy, warm sensation that comforts me. I have a sciatic problem, and I feel much better since I am using it four days a week. It also relaxes me and gives me a positive attitude for my daily routine." *X.V., FL*

"I believe it has improved my memory, helped me to remain balanced, to not gain as much weight as I otherwise would have, to retain a youthful appearance, to have more strength and energy, to reduce stress in my life, and to get the rest and sleep I need." *D.D., VA*

"I am 73 years old and have been using the **RADIAC** since 1980. I find that it heals tension in the body and relaxes the mind, which has improved my memory. Also, I use it for better circulation since I lead a more sedentary life. It is good for arthritis too, of course. Also, using my more alert mind... I am more creative." *E.G., Deerfield, IL*

"I am very pleased with the results of the **RADIAC** after only one month. I have noticed increased strength in my arms and legs, plus the ability to sleep better. An intestinal fungus and bacteria have created systemic imbalance, but the **RADIAC** seems to counteract these negative influences." *D.P., Julien, NC*

"I have been using the **RADIAC** on a systematic basis for about a month and a half now. I found a small reference in the **RADIAC** file to menopause, so I started using it for that. I had a problem with prolonged bleeding which

I could tell was not a natural flow so I followed the suggestion to place the negative lead just above the pubic bone and the positive on the "fourth lumbar plexus." It stopped the flow with one treatment, but the next day the bleeding began again. It stopped again with another **RADIAC** treatment. So did the cramping and bloating. I have not had any problems as of this date. I truly believe that I will not have a difficult time with this stage of my life with the help of the **RADIAC**. Other benefits I have noticed are a wonderful calming of my mind and body every time I use the device. I feel 'recharged' as if I have my second wind." *S.D., FL*

"I purchased the **RADIAC** appliance for my son who has been diagnosed with A.D.D. He started using the appliance in May 1995 and saw improvement in his self control within a month. By July, other family members were commenting on how much Austin had changed and how much calmer he had become. The majority of these people were not aware of him using the appliance, and made the assumption that he must be maturing. When he returned to school last September, his teacher was very surprised to find how much his confidence and attention span had improved. ...from the moment we started using the **RADIAC** miracles took place. He is still the same child that I had a year ago, but he can control his body and mind more than he could before...a whole lot more. One of the most important things that I found with the appliance is that my 6 year old son is requesting nightly to have it put on, 'because it makes me feel good inside' he says." *C.B, NJ*

"I have been using the **RADIAC** now for about three weeks and have noticed a change in my overall health. I have suffered with depression since I was a teenager and have tried anti-depressants with various side effects. I wanted to get off the drugs and try something different. I feel better than I have in a long time and believe it is because of the **RADIAC** appliance." *L.M., CO*

"The Castor Oil packs are still important for me; they work like magic. The **RADIAC** is another magic with the [Vibradex®] Gold Solution. It feels like golden sunshine from inside out." *O. J., Iceland, Europe*

"The **RADIAC** has been fantastic for eliminating tension headaches. Especially works well for those headaches that aspirin or Tylenol can't touch! The **RADIAC** gets rid of very bad headaches in about 15 minutes. My thanks to you for making it available." *J. G., CA*

"I tingle at connections. Tingle in extremities. Tingle all over. The strongest sensation is in my weak leg. As days progressed I began to dream again, my thinking processes are becoming clearer and clearer, my memory recall is improving, my weak leg is strengthening." *M.S., VA*

"You guys saved my life with the **RADIAC** unit and special [Vibradex® #185] Solution for Lyme. Thank you so much!!" *C.D., O.R.*

"I was particularly interested in Edgar Cayce's explanation of dreams and the world of dreaming because I had always been a vivid dreamer and could easily bring dreams back with me when I woke. Exploring the readings about dreams uncovered the mysterious **RADIAC** appliance for me. I was just finishing my studies as an engineer and the idea of a body balancing apparatus was intriguing to me. I was also beginning a meditation practice at the time and so I thought it would be interesting. It wasn't until a few years later that I decided to bring the **RADIAC** into my dreaming and meditation practice. It just made sense that it should help connect the two in a deeper way. Cayce recommended dreams as the best way to meditate and meet with the higher self and along with that, the **RADIAC** was recommended.

"I honestly didn't know what to make of it, and I went into it with an open mind. The first few times I connected to the **RADIAC** it seemed like nothing. Then after a week or so of using the **RADIAC** in a contemplative mindset, I began to notice myself drifting off to sleep and waking up at exactly the time I wanted to remove it (almost to the second sometimes). I was always a deep sleeper, but now I began to notice something different in my sleep. I would dream the most amazing and profound dreams and wake up from them feeling as if I had gained some unbelievable insight or relief during the night. It wasn't uncommon to dream about people I knew who were dealing with some concern and have the solution presented in the dream. I would wake up energized from the experience!

"I thought to myself, 'why doesn't every body own one of these little guys!?' and I believe they should. I've been using the **RADIAC** on and off for many years now and it never fails to set the stage for a peaceful night of sleep full of useful and interesting dreams. A nice little side effect is that I no longer use an alarm clock and can seemingly wake up at will any time I want. I guess the **RADIAC** set my internal clock on track!

"I can't recommend the **RADIAC** enough for its wonderful supportive qualities to the mind and body and I'm glad you are making it available." *J.B., Olney, MD*

"I have been using the **RADIAC** daily. I look forward to the half hour sessions and have found the net effect so far to be very calming. I have had Chronic Fatigue since January 2001 and had to retire early and limit my activities harshly, which has caused a good bit of anxiety in my life as I am normally very active. The anxiety has been greatly reduced since using the equipment and my muscles seem to be more relaxed, reducing the associated pain in tendons and joints." *B.M., Austell, GA*

"I have been using the **RADIAC** following the pattern of application of 12 days followed by 8 days of rest as suggested in the **RADIAC** books. I have noticed that when the **RADIAC** receives direct sun during the day, I experience a feeling as of a transfusion of warmth after about 10 minutes of application. I was struggling with some depression before I started using it, but now the depression is gone. Thank you, your work is invaluable." *B.P., Concord, NC*

"I have had Lyme's disease for the past 10 years. I initially went to the doctor and had the starter pack of antibiotics. The antibiotics seemed to help, however the disease came back stronger than ever after about 3 weeks.

"I went to a leading infectious disease expert at a school of medicine.

"After $5000 dollars worth of checkups, tests and blood work, I was told I had depression and was prescribed anti-depressants. I suffered with headaches, joint pain, severe short term memory loss, fatigue, and severe shortness of breath. There were some days I would plan out what I wanted to do for the next few hours. If I didn't write it down, I would forget and wander around the house knowing I had something to do but couldn't remember what it was. There were some days I couldn't work for a couple of hours. Extreme fatigue would set in. If I sat down I would fall asleep for 10 or 12 hours and still be able to sleep when it came time to go to bed. I could not exercise past a brisk walk of a 100 yards without a coughing fit. The coughing fits were like having a bad case of bronchitis.

"I searched the web (Cayce's readings) for an alternative relief from the Lyme's disease and this is where I found a reference to the Vibradex® Solution #185 and the **RADIAC**. I ordered the **RADIAC** about 2 weeks ago. I used the **RADIAC** the first four day cycle without the solution and then took a few days off. I then did one four day cycle with the solution.

"The first cycle I noticed more energy and fewer less severe headaches.

"After the first day using the solution, I could already tell the solution was attacking the babesia or whatever causes the difficulty breathing. It was like taking the first round of antibiotics for bronchitis/pneumonia.

"The congestion started to break up and I could take a lung full of air without difficulty/coughing fits. By the end of the first cycle with the solution I felt better than I have for years, even with the side effect of the solution killing off the infection. I can't wait to continue using the **RADIAC** to finish off the lyme's disease.

"I have slept sounder/better, less fatigue, and greater mental clarity than I have in literally 10 years. I would recommend the **RADIAC** to anyone for improved sleep and more energy, let alone if they have had to suffer through the awful disease associated with Lyme's." *R.M., Taylorville, IL*

"I was showing off to some neighboring kids when I felt a rip which I though was my shirt. It wasn't my shirt but a leader in my arm. I was unable to move two fingers. That night I used the **RADIAC** appliance with silver solution in the jar. The next morning my arm was completely cured." *F.M., Henrico, VA*

"I have enjoyed using my **RADIAC** unit. I have found that it has really helped with the neuropathic flares that I was getting in my fingers and toes. They have nearly disappeared. I am also enjoying better, more restful sleep." *L.C., West Lafayette, IN*

"With **RADIAC**, the quality of my sleep has been greatly improved. I sleep really deeply like when I was a teenager. As my blood pressure is low, it took me a few hours to start functioning at my optimal level in the morning before **RADIAC**. But now, thanks to **RADIAC**, I am ready to go mentally and physically as soon as I wake up in the morning from my beauty sleep!" *M. T., Tokyo, Japan*

"We purchased 2 **RADIAC**s after hearing Bruce Baar at a seminar in St. Petersburg, Florida. At the time we had some uncertainty about this device as to how much could it do for us, but something seemed to guide us to try it.

"Even after bringing them home we had to adjust to the idea of connecting the appliance up to our body. I tried to believe that I did feel something going on in my body. I lay on the bed and went quiet, then meditated, which felt good. The next day, I thought I felt better. We continued to use the **RADIAC** late in the evening mostly 10:00 PM, leaving it on for 30 – 40 mins. By the fourth of fifth morning I knew I felt more energy, waking up feeling rested, and realized after each treatment that elimination was better.

"I have applied the **RADIAC** some 33 times since the beginning. After not using the appliance for maybe 3 days, I make sure I find time to apply it, as I notice I need some more energy to play golf, (always walking the course).

"I am 71 years and my husband is 79. We have just had physicals at our family doctor. He suggested that whatever we were doing – to continue with it. (We did not tell him we were using an appliance called **RADIAC**)." *I.J., New Port Richie, FL*

"I attribute the increase in intuition and calmness, understanding and patience to the unit. I try and use it frequently. I remember more flickers of dreams. Once in awhile I'll remember a lot of a dream." *D.F., Cincinnati, OH*

"I just wanted to let you know that I've been using the **RADIAC** since right after Christmas. My blood pressure was reading 189 over (I don't know what). Sometimes it would be 176, etc. After using the **RADIAC** one month my blood pressure was 132 over something... the nurse said it was normal. I just had my pressure checked at the end of April and it was 110/70.

"I've been a life long insomniac and I sleep pretty well now. I don't wake up all night long the way I always have.

"Also, when menopause hit I started loosing words. That is also better... not perfect but I do notice a difference." *J.A., Saint Marcos, TX*

"Thank you both for your assistance and guidance about the **RADIAC**. I have used it for 19 times now. I instantly felt the subtle power of it in my pulse points from the very first time I applied it. When I first unwrapped it, felt that a great deal of work had gone into making it, along with an infusion of positive healing energy. I have proof that **RADIAC** works as a health protection, too. Someone I spent a great deal of time with in close quarters over the holiday season had a bad cold, but miraculously I remained healthy and cold-free throughout the ordeal. (If only everyone would use a **RADIAC**!! Maybe that person will, at least.)

"Bless you, all of you, at Baar Products. Keep up the good work!" *K.C. N Hollywood, CA*

I've had and used my **RADIAC** for a month-end result-more energy – all my faculties are enhanced – I'VE ROUTED DEPRESSION, I'M EASILY MOTIVATED BY MYSELF. I've sometimes felt pulses in my chest. I use my **RADIAC** 4 days per week now – although I at first did a 16 day – 4 day at a time cycle." *B.S. Wellsville, PA*

"I have used the **RADIAC** 4 times, plain and twice with Vibradex® Gold . Also I used the Epson Salt Baths and Castor Oil Packs for Rheumatoid Arthritis. My sleep is more restful, mood elevation, joints more flexible with decrease in pain throughout my body. Am grateful and thankful for a loving God, and Edgar Cayce's obedience with divine knowledge to help others." *B.M.W., RN. Winston-Salem, NC*

"After using the **RADIAC** for a series of times I felt my nervous system 'breath a sigh of relief!' My inner stability seemed to be in balance to allow a more even flow of emotions and thoughts. I felt an 'edge' of tension was lifted and an inner sense of well-being became evident." *L.K., N Myrtle Beach, SC*

"I have been using the Baar **RADIAC** appliance for a few years. I enjoy the relaxation that comes over me as I am using the **RADIAC**. I use it for the 4 day cycle and noticed that my sleep improves and my energy level increases. It creates a balance within me which helps deal with daily living in a peaceful, calm manner." *K.S., Downingtown, PA*

"My first session was 30 minutes. I felt a really nice clear, smooth, light sensation throughout my body after I was done. Later that evening I had a spontaneous emotional release with powerful unstoppable crying for about 3o minutes - no thoughts - no reasons, just tears - then gone. It felt great.

"My next session the following day for 1 hour. This time I felt immediate flowing through my whole body throughout the session. Later that day my entire left side from my shoulders down were intensely sore. No physical reason, just old stuff my guess. By the next morning totally released and feeling great.

"The 3rd session again there was increasing awareness of the flow of energy in my body during a 30 minute session. Later, both my knees were very sore, but the next morning there was no soreness.

"I have now completed 2 whole cycles and my mind is quieter and my general sense of physical presence is powerful, clear an uplifted.

I look forward to deepening further progress. Great job on the production of the **RADIAC**." *J.M., Brattleboro, VT*

"I've only used it twice... both times I've felt extremely relaxed to the point of euphoria. My family says I've been calmer and more pleasant. I had a very spiritual dream after the second use." *P.R. Benson, AZ*

"My Radiac is new, I have only used it for one complete cycle, but I have experienced results already. My meditation time with the **RADIAC** is much more centered. I use the **RADIAC** in the morning and my day is noticeably more peaceful and centered. Your instructions are clear and easy to follow. Thank you." *M.C. Virginia Beach, VA*

"Although I have only done three **RADIAC** sessions I have huge improvements in clarity of dreams in meaning and clear pictures! Also I see more positive dreams that wake me up happier!" *K.X., Athens, Greece*

"The **RADIAC** is wonderful and everyone should have one! "I am a high-strung person who is usually too nervous to consider relaxing. When I hook on the **RADIAC**, it is only a few minutes before I go limp and I can feel my energy balancing throughout my body, especially in chakra areas. I also use it to mediate (which is not hard to do being so relaxed) and have found Cayce's recommended Bible excerpts to be inspiring. I love my **RADIAC**! Thank you Baar for making this amazing device available!" *J.E., Grand Rapids, OH*

"Even if I didn't take a soporific, I got possible to sleep. And my sleep was deepened and I wake by a refreshing feeling when morning comes. "I believe that my illness improves with Cayce reading and **RADIAC**." *T.N. Kamigyoku,Kyoto-Si, Japan*

"I bought the **RADIAC** appliance over 1 year ago. My use has been sporadic, but when consistent has contributed to more restful sleep, lucid dreaming/ dream recall, and when I have been very consistent, improved focus during meditation." *E.H., Knoxville, TN*

"I have just stated using the **RADIAC**. When using the appliance I experience a warmth throughout my body and a strong sense of peace. My concentration has improved. Dreams have become clearer and the ability to focus on detail has been superb. I am looking forward to many years of experimenting with the **RADIAC**." *A.R., Oak Harbor, OH*

"When using the **RADIAC** a deep sense of relaxation settles over my entire body. In activity I experience continuous deep transcendence and my meditation is more profound. My yoga practice is also stronger which indicates increased physical stamina, I have completed 3 cycles (12)." *P.J-M, Pinon Hills, CA*

"Since using the **RADIAC**, it has helped me enormously to relax. Early days yet, but to date the experience has been very positive." *K.N., Cork, Ireland*

"At first it seemed the results of using the **RADIAC** were not worth the inconvenience. However, after about 2 weeks use, I found myself to be calmer and move balanced, able to remain calm even during the workday at a high-stress health-care job. I am involved in a holistic regimen for hypertension & when using the **RADIAC** I get lower readings than when I get lazy & skip sessions. I also find I sleep better and feel more rested, and meditation is deeper & more effective when done during a **RADIAC** sessions. All in all, I feel the purchase of the **RADIAC** was one of the best decisions I've made." *K.L., Aliquippa, PA*

"I use the **RADIAC** during meditation for 30 minutes 4 times per week. I have noticed an unusual clarity during meditation. Also, when the red wire is connected to my left wrist, I notice a subtle energy from my left upper torso to the left side of my neck & head." *S.H., Frankfort, KY*

"I've been using the radial appliance and I love it. I feel more relaxed and alive. I've had a skin condition on my hands that comes up only during the winter time. I started using the appliance and this condition slowly faded away." *R.G., Tulsa, OK*

"I was suddenly stricken from Bells Palsy a few weeks ago. I firmly believe that the RADIAC has helped the acceleration of my recovery. Not only does it help with the healing of nerves but it also prevents and gets rid of muscle fatigue.

"The other day I played tennis for only an hour and a half and moved ONLY two things in the attic. I decided to NOT use the RADIAC to test out my theory. What a mistake! I was writhing in pain the next day. My joints hurt and my calves ached from crouching and moving stuff in the attic.

"After using the RADIAC last night I fell well again. This device is truly incredible!

"NOT only does is it a GREAT healing device, it improves dream retention. My dreams are more vivid than ever. After using the device I always look forward to sleeping." *T.M., Wahiawa, HI*

"Wonderful soothing relaxation. Relief of pain. Relief of headaches. Relief from fatigue." *D.C. Windsor, VA*

"I have done one full cycle with the **RADIAC** and each of the four sessions has been different. The first one was the most interesting-I went into a relaxed meditation-like state almost immediately and my stomach gurgled frequently during the 30 minutes (stomach gurgling is my body's 'voice'- it happens when I'm getting a massage or when I've had a very satisfying meal.)

"I've noticed a reduction in negative thoughts so far (I tend to brood over things) and just in general a more peaceful state of mind.

"One thing I wanted to mention (that you might consider adding to your direction booklet) is that a person should be well hydrated before their **RADIAC** session (which means drinking plain water.) The body generates the bio-electricity that the **RADIAC** uses and this requires sufficient hydration for the ions in the blood to flow.

"I also have a question: Why do the electrodes need to be cleaned after the **RADIAC** is used? It makes logical sense to use the emery cloth to create a good contact before attaching them to your skin but I can't figure out what cleaning them after a session is supposed to accomplish. (I do this step anyway, just to follow procedure.)" *L.M., Tolland, CT*

"The **RADIAC** with the gold solution is amazing! The first night I used it I had a dream which solved a lifelong personal problem. The third night, I had a dream which helped solve a medical problem. It has also tremendously helped my energy and memory. This is a God send! Thank you." *C.B., Encinitas, CA*

"I have used the **RADIAC** 4 times so far-and noticed I seem to have more energy-I will keep using it." *V.A., Golden, CO*

"The half hour I spend attached to the **RADIAC** is the most relaxing of my day. I don't know that I sleep but I leave everyday thoughts & concerns behind. I've been doing 3 or 4 cycles then a break of 4 days." *J.S., Romney, WV*

"As a long term (13 years) Parkinson's disease patient, I personally believe that my daily 'good time periods' (on) had grown shorter while the bad 'off periods; had lengthened.

"Now, at the end of my second **RADIAC** cycle my perception is that the quality of both times has improved." *W.F., Harlingen, TX*

"I found that I sleep very well with the **RADIAC** and that my timing to run into people for helpful reasons increases." *F.O., Englewood, NJ*

"It seems to have greatly improved my acid reflux. And when I first tried it, my left arm which I was having some issues with, tingled during the treatment. So far I have only done 4 days." *T.B., Richardson, TX*

"When I first received my **RADIAC** appliance I was a bit apprehensive about using it because of its spiritual aspect, so I did not apply it for a week. I would set it in the sun, then chicken out.

"After placing it in the sun to charge I picked it up and knew instantly that we were going to be good friends because of the warm glow I received after holding it for a few moments. Then I applied it and WOW.

"I will try to explain. After hooking myself up, about ten seconds after I laid back and relaxed I could feel a force moving through my energy body and straight to my solar flex region then my energy body doubled up as if it had been punched in the solar flexes. I could almost imagine my energy body saying, 'what the heck is going on.' Then it began to relax and I could feel the **RADIAC** energy flowing through out my energy fields, then I began to get slight headaches for short periods of time in various parts of my mind after which I started grinning the biggest cat shire cat grin you have ever seen and I could not stop smiling... then I remembered to 'come in with expectations' and I started a meditation routine of relaxing each of my body parts in turn. I was doing that, almost instantly, I could feel each of the parts respond with the most pleasant of sensations. Then, all of a sudden my timer sounded and it was over with and the thirty minutes had passed in what seemed like three minutes.

"After disconnecting I laid there for thirty more minutes to allow for the rest period and the feeling of euphoria never left me. After I emptied the ice bucket and sanded the disc I went to sleep and I felt very alive and wonderful. I have the impression that I had the most amazing sleep experience but I cannot remember it.

"Day 2 - I hooked up, turned out the lights, laid back, relaxed and nothing happened for about ten minutes. To begin my meditation I had my forefinger and thumb connected and I had placed my tongue behind my upper front teeth to complete the three connections. At first I felt a little uncomfortable and slightly painful where the discs were connected, my left hand began shaking and I felt a pulsing and pumping sensation between my wrist and the disc. I could feel my pulse beating between my forefinger and thumb and at my right ankle. I was apprehensive and tense when I began the session so I started meditating and after ten minutes or so I began to feel a tingling sensation, very slight at first and it increased as time went on until I was tingling very strongly over my entire physical body and I began to energize as if I were a drained battery put on a charger.

"After about fifteen minutes I had a consciousness shift and the only way I can explain it is: it was like being at a movie when the reel quits running and the movie stops and everything goes black then the reel begins going again and the movie starts to play, slowly at first, then it speeds up to actual time. At the same time this was going on I had the sensation of falling into one of my other bodies as if the two make a connection some kind, (I feel into one of my other selves so to speak), with a sudden impact, I did not fall from the top down but I fell from the bottom up as if I was trying to catch up, it was a little shocking at first but not an unpleasant experience.

"I felt more conscious of time during this episode but after it was over with, again, it felt more like three minutes had passed instead of thirty. I don't know, but maybe I was experiencing time on two different levels simultaneously...

"During my meditation I asked that my fear, anger and anxieties be taken away. This morning I feel differently on all accounts. I am still getting the rushes of tingling sensations as I write this.

"Day 3 - I hooked up, turned off the lights, laid back, relaxed and three seconds later the alarm went off and it was over and nothing seemed to have happened. Thinking back I remember setting myself up for meditation and my right wrist began to burn where it was connected to the disc and again my left hand began to shake but not as badly as the day before and there was something going on at my right ankle where it was wired in but there was a slight pain in my left ankle if I remember right.

"I remember inviting my spiritual teachers to join me and we were in a room and for some reason I changed channels and began relaxing my body. Then a wooden door that appeared at the top, surrounded by flowers, closed. Shortly thereafter the alarm sounded.

"I have had a feeling of fulfillment and I have been very content all day. I have been very relaxed in my back a shoulder areas where I normally carry a lot of tension. While driving, my mind tried to become angry, which I suffer with, but something took over and I relaxed and let it go. For some reason I cannot get upset, be angry or carry a grudge. Contentment seems to be the word! This is very good stuff!

"Something else I have noticed, the AC in my house is malfunctioning and it runs wide open twenty four seven and the constant temperature is sixty six degrees, which is too cold for me. But, when I am wired into the **RADIAC** I never feel the cold and I am lying in bed wearing only my T-shirt and underwear. After I disconnect and relax in bed for my thirty minute rest period I begin to get cold.

"I think the secret to the **RADIAC** is when you begin a session to go in with expectations, tell it want you are trying to achieve what it is you expect to receive but be willing to give something in return. I asked to it to help me with my anger and now I cannot get angry, I am more relaxed and much calmer and I hope to be a more pleasant person for others to be with.

"Tonight I will ask to enjoy my life more and to be more enjoyable for others so they can enjoy their lives more in an out of my presence. I love my **RADIAC**.

"Day 4 - I hooked up, turned out the light, laid back, relaxed and nothing happened that I could tell. I really did not feel any sensations as I did during the other three nights. At one point I began OBEing a bit but did not quite make it out. I was at the threshold and I was seeing a dynamic pattern like energy radiating out from a central point in an oval shape (like an eye) but there were no colors. My body gave a couple quick powerful jerks that snapped me back in. I was more aware of the passage of time during this session but the time still passed pretty quickly... I slept peacefully and I had dreams but I do not remember any of them I just know that I dreamt and that they were powerful. Today I have been very peaceful and relaxed although I have had several angering incidents that I simply did not react to, which is good.

"My mind seems more unified and my emotions are tied in some kind of way that I cannot explain. I feel oddly, different as if I am not quite myself. I get the feeling/impression that something good is about to happen and all is well in my life and the world. I think the feeling is that of satisfaction and clarity of mind although I am still a little scrambled from last night's session." *D.W., Ft. Buchanon, PR*

"We have two **RADIAC**s, but have listed only one. My husband has had (very) high blood pressure, but now it's completely normal. We both sleep better and deeper. I'm remembering my dreams, and all of my body's elimination systems are working better. I've tended to retain water, but it is considerably less now. We are very happy with our **RADIAC**s." *R.W., Spokane, WA*

"About 12 years ago I was told about the **RADIAC**. It has been found helpful with arthritis and certain types of dementia. Since I was already experiencing some arthritic pain, and dementia is very prevalent in my family, I decided to give the **RADIAC** a try. The arthritis has not gotten any worse, and may have improved some. I have very little pain from arthritis. I am now 71. It may be a little early to say about dementia, but both of my parents were having problems before they were 71, and I do not seem to be having any problems yet." *D.G., Tupelo, MS*

"The first time I used it I could feel it working. The device reminds me of the feeling with acupuncture. I am sleeping more soundly and I have more energy during the day." *A.H., Pittsburgh, PA*

"I am happy to send you a testimonial about using the **RADIAC**. I have used mine, off & on, since 98/99(?). I have notice that when I use it, I can tolerate summer heat much more easily. And, in winter, I do not feel the cold a easily because my circulation improves. If I sprain a muscle, anywhere, especially in my back, I use the **RADIAC**.

"I am very familiar with energy flows, and it makes perfect sense to me that it re-distributes the energy that has become clumped via injury. I am really interested in the use that some have had with cranial energy flows, dementia, etc.

"I am grateful that you have been willing to invest your time in your company, making these items easily available." *J.C., Thornton, IL*

"I've only used the **RADIAC** for one cycle (4 sessions) but already I feel I have more energy and sleep better." *S.W., Midlothian, VA*

"About the time I was using my **RADIAC** regularly I did notice a remarkable improvement in my seasonal allergies. That was the only major thing I noticed, but it was a big thing to me. Spring and especially fall allergies used to drive me nuts. I could go through a big box of tissues a day. Sometimes a steroid shot would pull me through the worst, but the shot made me want to crawl out of my skin for 3 days.

"Well, I haven't needed the shot or the warehouse full of tissues in years." *G.M., Allentown, PA*

"I have enjoyed using the **RADIAC**. I find it provides a sense of peace. I go into a prayerful state while using it! Thank you for keeping the Edgar Cayce spirit in our lives." *L.H., Winthrop, MA*

"A few days before I had been sick (virus). It left me with an off balance-feeling in my head. Within maybe 5 to 7 minutes of using the **RADIAC** I felt a strong sensation centered forehead radiating out and to my eyes. This continued for the entire 30 minutes. Suddenly an inward explosion of light in right eye-my entire body jumped. It was great!

"Today, I feel great also. I know it was as good as what I had read. I feel a different kind of peace." *B.O., Rock Hill, SC*

"Thank you so much for your service, designing and selling holistic medicine recommended by the Edgar Cayce readings. I have used my **RADIAC** device for two cycles (eight sessions) and have felt only benefited by it... As I first attach the nickel dome anodes to the opposing planes of the body, I feel as if my body mind is"ignorant" of subtle energy. However, after the current is allowed to flow and 5 to ten minutes have passed, I feel a pacific whirlpool, or vortex of energy, around my lower abdomen, extending outside of my body, freeing up the chi energy and making me less ignorant of my chakra body. An interesting aspect of this balancing is that I literally feel more balanced, as if the right and left sides of my body are made symmetrical and are naturally relaxed." *S.M., Dedham, MA*

"I have been working with the **RADIAC** for several months now and have recently added work with a solution and solution jar. I find the entire process amazing. I could feel the energy immediately when I 'hooked up' to the **RADIAC**. My friends and family have noticed an improvement in my energy and even when speaking on the phone long distance people have commented on the improvement in energy in my voice and how I sound very positive and 'full of life.'

"After suffering a bad back injury which affected every part of me, the improvement in sleep, pain relief, flexibility, digestion, ability to walk for longer distances and to lift heavier things, and a feeling that it isn't the end of life as I once knew it after all, is so greatly appreciated. Also the use of the solution jar with iodine for my longstanding thyroid challenge (which runs in my family on both sides) has resulted in improved alertness, memory, energy, and even weight loss which is a challenge since my injury created an inability to exercise as I once did.

"In addition, I have meditated regularly for years and have found an improvement in my meditations and in the ability to go deeper, stronger and longer. Before a session with the **RADIAC** I pray and ask for help from all of the healing angels, healers, and helpers serving Earth's evolutions and specifically working with me in my life. I also ask for the Spirit of Edgar Cayce to guide this work and to help me know anything else I need to do to support this healing work within and without. I am very grateful for this opportunity.

"I am feeling much better and learning a lot in the process. I am grateful to God and all who love me in Spirit and in Matter for blessing me with the knowledge of the **RADIAC**, Edgar Cayce, Baar.com, and the Body/Mind/Spirit connection and for the opportunity to put what I have learned into action. 'Mind is the builder' and heart is the healer in me in co-creation with the Divine. I am very Grateful!" *A.A., Charles Town, WV*

"I bought the **RADIAC** as a sort of last desperate measure, because I'd had to quit working due to fibromyalgia, and I had very little money to support myself. However, I bought the unit, and after 20 treatments with gold chloride, I see that there is definite positive change in both my pain and flexibility levels. **RADIAC** is doing for me, in ONE MONTH, what the MD's couldn't do over 6 years!

"I am, of course, far from totally healed, but I'm so much better at this point that I'm positive I will be completely healed over a longer period of time. I am now, at age 62 (almost), starting a new e-commerce business for which I have high expectations. Thank you Mr. Cayce and thank you Baar Products for making this wonderful 'appliance' available!" *J.B., Pomona, CA*

"I just finished 2 cycles of the **RADIAC** and it gave me an incredible feeling in my solar plexus. I am 67 years old. The feeling was like being solid and centered in my solar plexus. A feeling of everything is good. Everything is right-words fail me on the feeling. Like a life force. A very good feeling. Everything is fine in the universe." *G.R., Madison, WI*

"I obtained a **RADIAC** at the A.R.E. Wellness Rejuvenation and Intensive. I have used it a few times since I have been home. I seem to remember better, when I loose something, I can visualize where the item is and then I locate it. I plan to continue using it." *C.W., Warwick, RI*

"I have experience a number of things since I started using the **RADIAC**. A reduced stress level; I have become much calmer and relaxed as noticed by family members as well as myself.

"My wife's aunt had originally thought the **RADIAC** might help with my RLS (restless leg syndrome), however, what I have found is that RLS is magnified during the **RADIAC** use.

"Prior to using the **RADIAC** (10 years plus) I have been using meditation to reduce stress and relax. While using the **RADIAC** and attempting to meditate I have found that I can't clear my mind no matter what, the **RADIAC** seems to be increasing the thought activity greatly. When I first started using the **RADIAC** it kind of scared me a bit, some of the thoughts I was having were a bit weird, like I have never had before. That has just about stopped now, but the increased mind activity during the session has not showed down at all.

"When I first started using the **RADIAC** I was feeling a slight shocking feeling on the skin of my arms and legs and sometimes in certain muscles. It is not as bad now but still happens occasionally.

"I am continuing to use the **RADIAC** and monitoring the various things that are happening." *J.E., The Woodlands, TX*

"I used the plain **RADIAC** for 16 days and couldn't believe the improvement in my sleep—right from the first day! I've used the **RADIAC** with gold & silver." *A.J., Silver Spring, MD*

"I had a peanut size lump in the arch of my foot. I've had this for at least 6 years. Since using my **RADIAC** I've noticed it's gone. (It was also very tender & sensitive.)" *J.W., Coon Rapids, MN*

"I have read many of the Casey books and have loved them, I've found great wisdom in all.

"I obtained the '**RADIAC**' and used it last night. I know it will improve me in all areas of health and I felt better on the first use... I've felt less fatigue and a good feeling all over." *E.W., Chalfont, PA*

"Linda's doctor said she had Peripheral Vascular Disease with a 70% blockage. Linda used the **RADIAC** for 6 weeks and then had a follow up Dr's appt. They were very surprised and said she should keep walking because her blockage went down to 20%. Linda does not do walking exercises and knows the **RADIAC** did this, so she uses the **RADIAC** all the time, now." *L.T., Dallas, TX*

"I was diagnosed with fibromyalgia in July, 2006. (I have also had chronic insomnia for years, and have taken between 100-150 mg. of Trazodone each night [enough to really 'knock out' most people for a long time!]). I retired from nursing in October, 2006, as my symptoms did not allow me to continue working. Nothing I have tried to relieve pain and debilitating fatigue have had any true beneficial effect. Western medicine is apparently at a loss to help fibro patients, and therefore provides no definitive treatment plan.

"I began my search with the Cayce remedies in the hope of finding something that would produce any type of relief. This led me to the **RADIAC** and your web site.

"I have had 3 'sessions' now with the appliance, and the results are extraordinary:

"I am sleeping deeply at night, a truly good sleep, and have cut my Trazodone dose in half. I am hoping to reduce it even more, with a goal of eliminating it altogether. In the morning, I am rested, and feel almost like a 'normal' person again, with a wonderful sense of well-being.

"This state of general well-being is also helping my muscle pain, which has been greatly reduced.

"Needless to say, I will continue with the **RADIAC** therapy!

"I am so grateful for the Cayce remedies, and so thankful to Baar Products for offering them, and especially for making available this truly amazing appliance." *C.F., RN, BSN, San Marcos, CA*

"The **RADIAC** lives up to its' billing. I find its primary effect is to relax tension throughout the body. Secondary effects include increased kidney function that sheds retained fluids.

"Recovery from exercise is enhanced and the body acts in a more youthful manner." *J.B., Hastings, NZ*

"I benefit greatly from the use of the **RADIAC** even though my usage is spasmodic - I am a poor patient and lack proper discipline when it comes to selfcare - much better treating others! Nevertheless it has proved a genuine life saver when all else has failed giving me vital energy to soldier on. ..." *C.M., London, GB*

"I've only had the unit for two weeks or so but I find myself craving the session. I enjoy an intense relaxation of my muscles within minutes of 'hooking up.' I've slept soundly all night for most of the last couple of weeks-which is unbelievable for me.

"I purchased this because my blood pressure is high." *L.S., Ontario, CA*

"The problem first began about 3 years ago while on vacation; lots of driving time and snacking, plus I've always been a 'big eater.' I have had mild pain in the left lower abdomen that would not go away. I've been an Edgar Cayce fan for decades so I am familiar with many of his diet suggestions and dream interpretations. I tried fasting, alkaline dieting to correct Ph as well as other diet suggestions for healing. Nothing made a permanent correction and the discomfort would always be back. I finally decided to try the **RADIAC** since it seemed to be recommended for deep seated health problems.

"The first night of the first four part session I had a dream: There was a large bare tree, even though I knew it was late in the season the tree produced beautiful new blossoms and growth. While quiet and meditating during the second of the first four part session, I saw a silver face and hand which prompted me to order the silver solution to use during future sessions. After the first few sessions I noticed that slight healing itch in the problem area, and have been pain free since.

"I can only offer my sincerest 'thank you' as well as deep admiration to the late Edgar Cayce, the A.R.E., Baar Products and the loving spirit of life that flows through all of you." *J.F., Grayslake, IL*

"I would like to let everyone I know exactly what the **RADIAC** has done for me, however I would like to share a little about what prompted me to purchase it.

"For my whole life I have suffered from anxiety attacks. The worst of these were in my 20s and 30s. actually taking myself to the hospital on several occasions. I can remember as a child of 6 or 7 feeling like I was in trouble for no reason.

"The last 10 years were not so bad as I am recovering from alcoholism (which I'm sure is a result of my anxiety) and will have been sober 10 years.

"Since the desire to stop drinking 10 years ago I had improved some, but the last 5 years my anxiety has picked several specifics to rear its ugly head. The first being I could no longer drive on the highway. I could not be a passenger in a car. I could not be in an enclosed room for meetings at work. I worried all the time about everything and nothing at all. I drive 40 minutes to work and take back roads to get there. Just thinking of going on the highway caused me to feel ill. I could no longer pull my horses let alone load them into the trailer. I was mentally a total wreck on a daily basis.

"I felt as if I were going to die at any moment (surely with a heart attack) knowing this stress I was suffering from was going to take me out that way regardless of what any doctor said. They all wanted to put me on antidepressants. Which I can not do because I am afraid to take medication. I had chest pains, trouble swallowing, and nervousness. I became breathless gasping for air. I was sure this was all because the anxiety but if I didn't do something about it, it was going to kill me.

"I remembered Edgar Cayce since I was a little girl my dad was fascinated by him. A year ago they had something on the history channel about 'the sleeping profit.' I recorded it and watched it over and over, for about a month. Then I started looking for him on the internet and A.R.E. However I couldn't get past the illness and the cures. Then I started researching a little more and found the **RADIAC**. I read about it over and over and over until finally I just had to try it. (I think God sent me here)!!!

"After 1 full cycle of the **RADIAC**, I was able to be a passenger in a vehicle. 'Heading down the freeway.' Not one time did I flinch, use imaginary brake or pin out of control in my mind. Actually I could not stop smiling because I was so pleased with my new ability. I drove home.

"My husband was more nervous waiting for me to (freak out).

"I have only used the **RADIAC** for 2 full cycles. And these are the results:

"Anxiety has dropped to almost nil, my depression has not returned, my whole attitude and out look has improved and I now look forward to my life (planning a trip to California in April) That's 2600 miles of highway that I haven't been able to see in 5 years and it thrills me to anticipate it where it used to make me physically sick. I feel more at peace and I don't like to push on anyone my spirituality. But I have more now than ever and am closer to God than I have been in my whole life. I now meditate and have the patience to do so. Today I am balanced.

"I will continue to use my **RADIAC** forever and will be getting my husband one as soon as I can." *D.T., New Castle, IN*

"With The Vibrational healing properties of the **RADIAC** appliance, along with several other factors, my girlfriend was able to get rid of her Lyme disease. Thank you for manufacturing a very ancient healing tool!" *C.M., Indianapolis, IN*

"This machine seems to work on the higher level chakras and has as far as we can tell, seems to help the body on levels we have not quite conceived of. If you remote view, it turbo charges your ability. If you are sending healing, it really powers this up as well. If you want to rest, it gives you a deeper level of rest.

"One of the theories is that it actually helps your body in future lives – tough to prove – but a good theory none the less. Meaning that if you are really working to keep your body clean, then the body in the next life may be a cleaner receptacle as well.

"I find that I cannot use it at night because I am supercharged I have to use it mid-day to get the best results.

"I can only use it once a week, or I cannot sleep at night, so something is happening, I think to the auric structure. Perhaps that means that the structure is more charged than it might have expected.

"I love it. I think it is a great machine." *T.E., La Mesa, CA*

"I have found the **RADIAC** to have a relaxing effect on my body. It seems to 'normalize' my body with regular use." *K.G., Reno, NV*

"I have been a meditator for 20 years and have always been irritated by the body. Since using the **RADIAC** the body discomfort has diminished greatly, therefore, I have experienced greater depth and more peaceful meditations." *M.C., Adelaide, S. Australia*

"My interpretation of this unit has changed my mental status dramatically. I am visual, mentally and physically healthy. This is as dreams come true." *N.B.T., Suwanee, GA*

"I have had restless leg spasms since 1968 which had been getting worse. After the third use of the **RADIAC**, there were no further spasms. I had been on sleeping pills for ages. I did sleep one night without pills thru night." *W.M., LaJolla, CA*

"Experience with **RADIAC**: It is amazing, I have more energy and my sleep improved (I don't need eight or more hours to sleep anymore in order to feel full of energy)." *M.R., Montreal, CA*

"My first experience was awesome. When I first started the process I felt a surge of energy come straight down the middle of my head to my stomach. I felt I felt sort a dryness. My stomach feeling little upset. Then as time went on I felt a tingling in both my hands. After it was over I felt somewhat serene. My head felt cleared and in somewhat an altered state.

"Been using the **RADIAC** for a couple of weeks now. I still get some good results but the most besides being relaxed is the dreaming I've been having. I'm remembering more plus they are so vivid. Dreaming a lot. If I wake up and fall back to sleep I start dreaming right away... Really good experience." *T.W., Clinton Twp., MI*

"My sleep seems deeper and my dreams are more vivid. I'm noticing more energy and stress reduction the days following my **RADIAC** sessions. A most significant benefit is a strong reduction in chronic pain in my neck, shoulders and upper back. On a subtle energy level I enjoy the sensations in the body the wild buzzing. It seems to continue even after the session is done." *A.C., Chicago, IL*

"After receiving the **RADIAC** and just finishing my 3rd rotation I thought I would let you know how things turned out.

"A quick intro in history – I've recently have had a mental and physical break-down due to enormously stressful events in my life. The past 2 months I have been in a physical and mental decline. I started (and still am) vigorously searching for inner healing and enlightenment, hence why I began to study and introduce Cayce remedies into my daily life.

"I'm an anti-pill person and have always known that the 'healing' can come from within, I just didn't know how, or perhaps lacked the patience to pursue.

"My first day's use of the **RADIAC**, I followed the instructions, laid on my couch, put on some headphones and listened to ambient music... After 30 minutes of meditation, I cleaned and stored away the **RADIAC**.

"Roughly 2 hours later, I realized that I did not experience the heavy "weight" that I had for the past 2 months – I felt a little lighter on the feet. It was not a magic bullet and cured all ailments, but, something happened and it was positive. I experienced the same yesterday after my second usage. Again, same result! I know I have a long way to go as I can still feel a deep penetrating depression, sluggish, lack of energy. But the **RADIAC** has done its job and I am slowly recovering (better to go up than down!).

I just wanted to thank you for your product. The **RADIAC** was a proper investment and I'm happy I made the purchase." *C.A., Ephrata, PA*

"Just a note to share my experience with the **RADIAC**. My reason for purchasing the **RADIAC** was not for any medical/health-related condition, but for energetic alignment. I am so pleased with the results!

"The first feeling that I experienced can only be described as: a feeling that there was no room in my heart for stinginess, pettiness, or any negativity/ diminishment of another being. I could no longer tolerate those qualities in other people or situations, and I now have to energetically separate myself. The **RADIAC** seemed to build up my energetic (psychic) resistance, stamina and made me not so susceptible to the feelings and energy of others – I think that I was not stable within my own energy, too easily overcome by the energy and feelings of others. Now I am grounded and stable within myself.

"Use of the **RADIAC** brings an overriding feeling of tranquility and happiness that weaves itself into all that I do - it is a feeling that 'All is well.' The feeling has made realize that worry is a choice and that I should just choose the better feeling that is being offered. In appreciation." *N.P., Chagrin Falls, OH*

"The **RADIAC**: It is amazing. I feel tingly all over and as if I am out of my body; completely at peace and I feel relieved and positive after; overall I feel better in body, mind and spirit. It is the best investment I have ever made for you and your well being." *Case #137168, T.T., Virginia Beach, VA*

"First time I felt a tingling feeling where the plates touched the skin. Right wrist and left ankle. My crown chakra opened and energy felt as if it passed through me. First session 1 1/2 hours and I feel centered with a tingling in my finger tips. Very Cool!" *W.C., Hicksville, NY*

"This **RADIAC** product helps me sleep better and promotes a gelling of well-being. I have Parkinson's Disease and this product helps me relax. I also notice I don't shake and move as much as I use to." *R.C., Rensselaer, NY*

"I am 53 years old, a recovering alcoholic for nearly eight years. Alcoholism runs in my family and encouraged the suicide of my only sibling 22 years ago. I have been an A.R.E. life member for a long time. When I first read about the **RADIAC** I thought it sounded funny and promising. However, I knew that I would be hard-pressed to stop drinking for four consecutive days, and that is how I initially read the instructions for the full cycle of using the **RADIAC**.

"It wasn't until I had stopped drinking for about six months... that I thought again of using the **RADIAC**. My agitation was profound. I had a very clear clenched-teeth, bitter emotional state of mind and heart.

"I ordered and used the **RADIAC**. The next day I found myself singing, literally. I was singing about walking down the stairs, singing about getting into the car. Even though I do talk to myself a good deal, I noticed this new way of being and realized that it was connected to my use of the **RADIAC**. I have continued using the **RADIAC** for a full cycle about every three weeks. The difference in my emotional state is always noticeable and always positive. I become happier, seemingly for no reason. It's easier to be in the moment and appreciate the tiny, beautiful aspects of life. It feels like there's a compassionate hand on my shoulder, letting me know everything is alright." *D.K., Portland, OR*

"The first night I wore the **RADIAC**, I noticed movement in my ankles and legs. I no longer suffer with RLS (Restless Leg Syndrome). What a great relief.

"After 8 days of use, I am beginning to notice movement in my head. I use it every night. I have more energy and I am not snacking as much. This appliance is great!

"I convinced my sister to order one and she's anticipating its arrival soon." *C.D., Lansing, KS*

"I definitely felt 'energy' at the pulse points on my wrist and ankle when applying the **RADIAC** for the first time. I know I'm in for an interesting journey." *T.L., Hixson, TN*

"I first began using **RADIAC** sometime in February, about three months ago. I only use it about four times a week, or sometimes five, depending on if I can find the time. There have also been weeks when I haven't used it at all, if I've been away from home.

"The first time I ever used the **RADIAC**, I felt an immediate, subtle pulse through my wrist with the red wire. The side with the black wire was harder for me to sense. The next day maybe the same.

"For about the first week, just walking around during the day (not connected to the **RADIAC**), I felt subtle, slightly awkward feeling. I could feel myself being 'rewired,' my right and left sides being adjusted somehow. I felt slightly out of sync in the exact same way as when I've done "Brain Gym" or yoga exercises like touching your right hand to your left knee, etc. I could almost feel something going on in my brain, a confusion. I even found it a bit hard to concentrate, maybe a little like jet lag.

"A decade ago, before I married, had children and moved to the West Coast, I studied Shiatsu at a Japanese style massage school for two years. So I know all about meridians and acupuncture points (though I've never in my life had acupuncture). I'd been told by more than one shiatsu practitioner that my right meridian is much stronger than my left. This is probably because I'm one of these people who is very 'right' handed – I use my right hand for almost everything. Occasionally I try to exercise my left side by using the computer mouse with my left hand, etc., but I tend to get very busy and forget.

"I do think the **RADIAC**, to some extent, has been helping to correct this 'right/left' imbalance.

"The strongest feelings came a few months ago. For sure, I felt results. Aside from that 'crossed signals' feeling with my brain, I do think that I was having better sleep cycles.

"My brother has his own **RADIAC**. He said that in the beginning he felt absolutely nothing and over time, after the first few weeks, or month, the **RADIAC** gradually began to work for him." *K.K., Seattle, WA*

"Since using the **RADIAC**, my daily vitality has increased. I have more energy during my workouts. My teeth have also strengthened! My dentist even told me that my teeth are strong. In the past, I was always told otherwise!

"Thank you for such a great product! I've only used it 32 days, and will no doubt continue to use it for the rest of my life." *J.L., Fremont, CA*

"The first time I used the **RADIAC**... I felt the energy (if that's what it is) immediately, starting at my feet. So I closed my eyes and allowed my Heavenly Father to show me things. I will share two images he has shown me because I hope they will bring you the same sense of joy and wonder.

"The images were beyond mere pictures but actual real places somewhere else, as real as any sights and sounds you might see or hear or feel. He showed me a beautiful tree being blown by a gentle breeze coming towards me... the long branches swaying so peacefully and gently, like on a summer day. It was a simple image but real... and brought me joy.

The second place... was to a French country estate with a very large long rectangular garden bordered by tall trees. A very sunny day. He placed me above a garden pool of black water and showed me the pool from which I could observe the gardens stretching very far to the east. Directly behind me was the Chateau. The pool was shaped like a circle and a square combined. At first I was apprehensive, because the water was black, but my concerns eased, and he directed my gaze eastward, and felt safe.

"Both visits to these beautiful places were brief, yet lasting, and return to my remembrance when it pleases the Holy Spirit to do so, and each time I am reminded of them they feel like special gifts from him to me."
T.S., Vancouver, WA

"I am currently experimenting with and using the **RADIAC** appliance.

"I also suffer from Graves disease (hyperthyroid) – my heart beats are very fast and my thyroid produces an over excessive amount of hormone.

"When I have fast heart palpitations I have used the **RADIAC** and instantly it has regulated my heart beats back to normal. I feel very good during the **RADIAC** treatments. I will keep you up to date with my future **RADIAC** treatments as well." *G.M., Fenton, MO*

"I love my **RADIAC**! I find it very relaxing- even when I am quite stressed. Sometimes I use it when I can't sleep. It seems to help me get more centered. After i use it I feel refreshed and more awake – as if waking up from a restorative nap. And, of course, it seems to help me meditate much more deeply." *B.D., Minneapolis, MN*

"I heard from my friend yesterday, he got the plain **RADIAC** without solutions. He said that the doctor was unable to tell which knee had been injured, since the severed ligament healed so cleanly. The doctor didn't believe that he got the injury a month ago. Thanks!" *I.Q., Inglewood, CA*

"There is no condensation on top of my **RADIAC**, which is another big improvement over the old 'Lester' units. Also, I am more energetic and I am dreaming again." *A.L., Los Lunas, NM*

"I feel like I sleep better with the **RADIAC**. Which in turn gives me more energy. My eyesight seems to have improved as well. I am 49 years old and considered to be in good health." *A.B., Shingle Springs, CA*

"Right from the very start, the **RADIAC** did improve my sleep [which was one of the main reasons I bought it]. I find myself sleeping more soundly and if I do wake up during the night I can fall back to sleep right away. Which was a problem for me before using the **RADIAC**.

"I also share some of the other experiences of people that was given in the **RADIAC** book. I feel more relaxed and calmer. And as I'm using the device I feel a tingling or prickling sensation mostly on my left side... sometimes my hands get warm. I'm looking forward to continued use of my **RADIAC**. I think the more it is used, more of its benefits are experienced." *F.H., San Diego, CA*

"I bought the **RADIAC** a while back to help with arthritis. It helped a lot. It gave me more energy, a feeling of well being, and I slept great at night without waking several times in the night (as I usually do). The pain resolved too. Thanks for making this product!" *J.K., Memphis, TN*

"I feel a personal attachment to my **RADIAC**. After use, my dreams seem more intense/real. The device seems to calm my anxieties." *B.G., Southhampton, NJ*

"For several years I have seldom been able to remember my dreams. The first night after I used the **RADIAC,** I started having vivid dreams which I now remember and write down right away. Also, I now wake up 15-30 minutes before my alarm each morning, feeling refreshed and ready to go." *L.D., Fall River, MA*

"I've used the **RADIAC** for a week now and I have slept great which is unusual for me. The first time I used **RADIAC** I notice a psychological affect that was very positive. Thank you very much for the **RADIAC**."

R.B., Sweetwater, TN

"I am amazed that after just two sessions [with the **RADIAC**], my leg pains have all but disappeared. What a relief!" *L.C., Bellaire, MI*

"It's possible that using the **RADIAC** has helped me in some recent enhanced accessing of the Life Force (which I also relate to each one's personal "intentionality"). Particularly during a recent night's half-sleep I experienced a certain, more open and less conditioned, so more powerful, of aliveness. I am variously reaching almost always to have ever more of this (and other basic elements of our psyche) – ultimately to ever better partnering with God, so to ever greater health, creativity, happiness, and on – and the **RADIAC**, particularly with solutions, is a part of this." *J.C., Albuquerque, NM*

"After my first session with the **RADIAC** I noticed I had more feeling in my left big toe, and new feeling in the toe next to it. After my sixth session, my gluts felt like they were on fire! That is good news because they have had minimal feeling for over a year. I believe the sessions combined with my physical therapy will help regenerate my glut muscles over the long haul, as they have constantly felt hot since that 6th session.
"Around the 12th session, I felt my right hamstring get warm sensations. Those feelings are the first I've had there since I got hurt [years ago]. Thankfully, they have also continued to feel warm.
"I'm very happy with these results & will continue to make progress!
"Thank you very much!" *R.G., San Antonio, TX*

"I purchased the **RADIAC** to address two potential health issues identified via blood tests taken over the past two years. The first concern I want to address is an increased level of creatinine (kidney function related) and worsening indicators for rheumatoid arthritis. During this two year period I took herbal supplements as anti-inflammation support but stopped the supplements the second year and started traditional medicine for anti-inflammation support.
"The major dietary change since beginning **RADIAC** therapy is a significant reduction in alcohol consumption. Previous to using the

RADIAC, I would have a glass of beer with my evening meal; however, I now have a beer only once or twice between treatments. The beer was usually dark and micro-brewed.

"Below is my nightly log for two cycles of **RADIAC** therapy.

"Cycle 1-1: Sinus or head cold with non-productive cough; wife sick, too. Taking colloidal silver. Burning sensation in right groin likely associated with ureter or kidney; previous kidney stones on right side. Immediate upon starting **RADIAC**-only therapy, there was a 'popping' like plastic bubbles bursting in left knee that is still stiff from past injury/surgery. Sensations eased after first 5 minutes.

"Cycle 1-2: Some discomfort in right ankle at contact point after ~25 minutes; discomfort passed within a minute or two.

"Cycle 1-3: Sinus much improved before treatment. Used cough syrup to inhibit cough beginning after 1st treatment and nothing since bedtime last night. Feeling better.

"Cycle 1-4: Nothing to note during the evening session but my face complexion seems to be improving.

"Prior to beginning the next cycle; I waited 10 days.

"Cycle 2-1: Sore from a lot of work in attic Sat-Mon. Sinus swollen from attic stuff.

"Cycle 2-2: Not feeling well today but better before session. Doc says he believes early stages of rheumatoid arthritis. Sinus trouble still. Fell asleep. As usual, breathing seems more refreshing afterwards. Left sinus still swollen.

"Cycle 2-3: Feeling normal today. Fell asleep last 15-20 minutes.

"Cycle 2-4: Feeling ok today but some limping because of left knee; resuming normal level of medication. Storms in the area today.

Now that I am familiar with **RADIAC** therapy, I plan to start a gold solution beginning next full cycle start in about 10 days." *D.P., Huntsville, AL*

"I've now been using the **RADIAC** for 2 years and feel rebalanced, energized, and calm after each use. It's just like I've had an acupuncture treatment, but in the privacy of my home. Truly amazing." *K.W., La Mesa, CA*

"I can fall asleep much easier when using Baar's **RADIAC**. I have very vivid dreams and don't wake up as many times during the night. When I wake up in the morning I remember my dreams and feel more energized then normal." *M.C., West Chester PA*

"I just used the **RADIAC**. This is my first use. I felt nothing then I felt tingling in my right fingers and left foot. After finishing with the **RADIAC**, my brain felt better, cleared, and my mood felt lifted. I feel happier. I feel like I have a wonderful day ahead of me and I can do projects and things…" *J.G., Shasta Lake, CA*

"I have used both Cayce appliances for several years, and I consider both to be invaluable. I urge every potential user to read everything she or he can on their instruction and proper use because, used correctly, they can and will benefit any condition." *S.W., Charlotte, NC*

"I bought a **RADIAC** about 4 years ago. It's been a God send. I use it often while meditating." *R.S., St. Louis, MO*

"**RADIAC** deepens my meditations, promotes a feeling of well being, deep relaxation. I really enjoy using it." *D.H. Sicklerville, NJ*

"I've completed three 4-day cycles with the **RADIAC**. My heart palpitations have lessened which is a big relief." *B.R., Liberty Lake, WA*

"I have 'sold' a chiropractic office on your products – especially since the **RADIAC** I got is making changes so noticeable to my chiropractor!" *D. H., Toledo, OH*

"…. Bless you, I really like my **RADIAC**. It is the best thing around, nothing compares." *E.B., Virginia Beach, VA*

"I fall asleep [with the **RADIAC**] within a few minutes of attaching it. I have used it everyday for a couple weeks now. All my senses became stronger after the very first usage... I have a cervical curvature that is being treated by the chiropractor and an extension cushion to stretch out my neck. The vertebrae involved is CV#1 & CV#2. The **RADIAC** must be pushing some energy through their and opening that up. I have PTSD (Army Veteran). ... I feel like a psychological drug has been administered and I am sedated, but it's natural in this case. A calmness I haven't felt since I was a child is being remembered in my body, and I can feel the effects of this powerful de-stressing. I will continue with the **RADIAC**." *B.K., Ft. Myers, FL*

"... After using the **RADIAC**, my leg was stronger. The congestion I had left, and I had a great attitude the next day." *D.D. Burlington, WI*

"The first time I used the **RADIAC** I had a wonderful experience. It brought me much peace and relaxed me over some issues that I was dealing with mentally. Thank you, and God's blessing be with you." *M.B., Dallas, TX*

"I felt less depressed and had more energy after using it. I also was much more relaxed while I was on it." *R.S., Travelers Rest, SC*

"I have used my **RADIAC** 3 times and have felt some vibration moving in my body while it is on, followed by a sense of deep relaxation & sense of well being. I am so glad to have finally purchased one after years of indecision." *C.V., Thetford, VT*

"I immediately feel a stillness, a stability, a calm that leads to peace and a sense of oneness. It is a meditative experience.

"Physically, I periodically experience warmth or energy throughout ... Additionally, I've experienced more vivid and lucid dreaming... I am eager to continue with these experiences and see if they change over time. I am keeping a journal to monitor these as well as my dreams." *P.L., Caseyville, IL*

"...I can tell I'm not as nervous. My hands & feet are warmer. I feel it will be beneficial looking forward to use again." *L.W., McKinney, TX*

"I have been using the **RADIAC** for a few months... My body feels very relaxed and I have a feeling warmth in my hands & feet at times. I've also felt a floating sensations of my body. The surprising thing that I found is that my hair was getting a bit thicker, curlier and less grey. The **RADIAC** certainly works its magic." *T.N., Marlton, NJ*

"I felt a gentle tingling sensation in my feet, which slowly spread through my body. It felt like a great acupuncture treatment! My body felt relaxed and lighter. I've only used it twice so far, but I plan to use it once a day for mediation and relaxation." *K.C. Kaneohe, HI*

"The **RADIAC** is a wonderful product from Baar! It has enhanced my life in so many ways! I sleep deeper, I dream deeper & my dreams are vivid! I feel as though I have so much more energy than I did prior to owning my **RADIAC**! Thank you so much Baar! *D.S., Burlington, NC*

"My wife has Fibromyalgia. She uses the **RADIAC** to help with mental clarity and sleep. She does 12 rotations in a row then four day rest." *J.C., Johnson City, TN*

"After using my **RADIAC**, my energy and metabolism have speeded up. Also, I haven't slept this well in my life, not even when I was a child. I'm a residential window cleaner and healer, and I am amazed with the **RADIAC** and all my improvements from using it." *C.C., Mountain Home, NC*

"I am deeply grateful for this device. I use it almost every day, improvements are numerous. Ease of breathing, energy, calmness…" *J.S., Boone, NC*

"I used my **RADIAC** the second day I had it, and the very first thing I noticed was a sense of calm. I hooked it up and lay there, and apparently I passed out. I had set a timer for 30 minutes. The next thing I knew I was waking up to the alarm and I felt very peaceful. I am really looking forward to tomorrow's session. Also, as I went for my afternoon walk, I felt more energized." *R.G., Summerfield, FL*

"Dear Dr. Baar, I have used the **RADIAC** and I have noticed a great improvement with my anxiety. When a confrontation at work arises, I feel I am less nervouse and much less stresed. I feel very confident and calm. I am also able to sleep better than before. I believe I have never felt this great! This is an easy and non-invasive way to balance mind, body and spirit. The radiac is just what I needed and look forward to my time using it!" *R.L., Dallastown, PA*

"I have used the Radiac for one 4-day cycle and I feel very good. By the third day, I was slipping off to sleep just when the timer went off at thirty minutes. I popped up refreshed." *J.C., Logan, OH*

"I did a session of 30 minute Radiac therapies for 4 days in a row. I feel more at ease and in control. Also, I feel Healthier and balanced. I am even sleeping better! I am pretty amazed with the results. The Radiac is my new best friend!" *S.J., Newport, RI*

"WOW! I've had an immediate effect from my Radiac. I think we will become the greatest of companions. It's like a loving mother, keeping you nurtured and whole." *L.O., Edinburgh, United Kingdom*

"Thank you. I am enjoying my RADIAC. I am having better sleep and deeper meditations. I'm also remembering my dreams :)" *D.R., Stockton, CA*

This information is for educational purpose only. It is not intended to diagnose, treat, cure or prevent disease. Statements contained herein have not been evaluated by the Food & Drug Administration, as in all health situations, qualified professionals should be consulted.

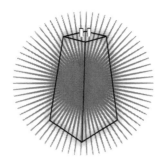

RADIAC® TRAINING

Contact Baar Products, Inc., for RADIAC training.

Telephone: 1-610-873-4591
Fax: 610-873-7945
Website: www.baar.com

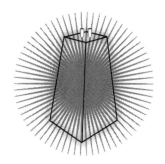

Index

PERSONAL NOTES

PERSONAL NOTES

Made in the USA
Middletown, DE
25 January 2017